Spelling instruction that makes sense

JO PHENIX/DOREEN SCOTT-DUNNE

Pembroke Publishers Limited

© 1991 Pembroke Publishers Limited
538 Hood Road
Markham, Ontario
L3R 3K9

Canadian Cataloguing in Publication Data

Phenix, Jo
  Spelling instruction that makes sense

Includes bibliographical references.
ISBN 0-921217-68-4

1. English language – Orthography and spelling – Study and teaching (Elementary). I. Scott-Dunne, Doreen.   II. Title.

LB1574.P54 1991   372.6'32   C91-094830-5

Editor: Joanne Close
Designer: John Zehethofer
Cover photograph taken at Regal Road Public School
  by Ajay Photographics
Typesetting: Jay Tee Graphics Ltd.

Printed and bound in Canada
9 8 7 6 5

We dedicate this book to Chris Worsnop and to Morna Scott-Dunne, both of whom have enabled us to grow as teachers and as writers.

Chris shared with us his love of language, and helped us to see the magic of words. He stimulated our interest in spelling by sharing his knowledge and experience. He encouraged us, along with many other teachers, to become researchers in our own classrooms, to link theoretical knowledge with our observations of students at work, and to write about what we learned. This book is one result of that experience.

From before the time she started school we have watched Morna grow as a writer and as a speller. She is a talented writer and poet, whose ability to use language far outstrips her ability to spell, as indeed it does with all young children. She has an instinctive appreciation of the place of spelling in the writing process, and has never allowed a lack of spelling knowledge to interfere with the joy of composition. Morna has shown us that the writing processes of a young child are not very different from our own, that writing and learning to write are not two different stages of development.

We wonder that it has taken us so many years of teaching to discover that we can learn equally from an adult expert and from a child.

Contents

To Teach or Not to Teach

When we both started teaching, the Friday spelling test was an almost universal event in our elementary schools, as much a part of the classroom ritual as the National Anthem. On each day of the week, prescribed exercises in spelling took place in preparation for this test. On Monday, the previous week's words could be abandoned as students prepared for the next list of random words. Three times a year, parents all over the province were reading in their children's Report Cards that "spelling is improving, but there is no carry over in the writing". In due course we realised that this kind of memorization game was not teaching our children much of worth about spelling.

At the same time, we began using a new and more liberal approach to writing in our schools. Instead of prescribing topics and focusing almost exclusively on the accuracy of spelling, grammar and punctuation, we shifted our focus to composition and creativity. After an initial period of wariness, our students wrote as never before. The quantity increased, the topics proliferated, the language and vocabulary knew no bounds as students were freed from the tyranny of marking.

A similar revolution was taking place in our reading periods, as we moved from controlled vocabulary and stilted texts to real children's literature, from total teacher control to independent reading and shared responsibility. Reflection and personal response took the place of written comprehension questions.

Those of us who have been involved in this return to natural language learning and real-life language experiences are in no doubt that our students have become better readers and writers and more proficient users of language as a result. Research has taught us a lot about how children learn, about how language is learned, about what kinds of experiences are necessary for successful learning. The rigid, old methods had to give way to new approaches which more closely match real-life experience.

There are, however, many misconceptions about what we ought to be doing in our classrooms. For example:

- "Whole language" means you should not teach phonics.
- Because personal writing is so important, we must never assign writing topics.
- Focusing on composition means you do not worry about spelling and neatness.
- We should not use words like "noun" and "verb" anymore.
- Whole-class instruction is wrong.
- Words to be learned should always come from the students' writing.
- Reading and writing will teach children all they need to know about spelling.
- We do not need to teach spelling as a subject.

The skills we want our children to learn have not changed. We want them to be good users of language in all its forms, written and oral, receptive and expressive. As a result of our new understandings about language learning, we have widened our goals. We put a premium on content in writing, and teach our students to work as real writers do, through a process of drafts and revisions. We value real substance over superficial accuracy. We try to respond to their efforts in a supportive way, and encourage experimentation and risk-taking.

None of this means we need to exclude a focus on spelling. Spelling is a part of the writing process, a part of life. Once our students feel free to write, have something to say and language to express their ideas, then we must teach them how to present their writing in standard forms of spelling. Quantity writing is only part of the learning process; helping the students learn as much as possible through this writing must be our goal in the classroom.

It seems to be a common misconception that schools and teachers no longer value or teach correct spelling. We know this is not true. Certainly other aspects of writing now receive more emphasis than before; composition is given its due priority as the heart and soul of the writing process. Spelling, however, has a vital role to play. We need to strike a balance in our teaching so that students understand the place of spelling, and have enough confidence as spellers that they are not inhibited as writers.

1. An Introduction to Spelling

The Mythology of Spelling

There are a number of myths supporting the belief that spelling cannot be successfully taught or learned. These myths need to be dispelled.

Some people can spell and some people can't, and that's the way it is.

There is no parallel myth that there are people who can read and people who can't, and there is not much we can do about it. It is certainly true that some people have more trouble with spelling than others. We don't give up on people who cannot read, so why should we give up on those who cannot spell?

People who see themselves as poor spellers often have not made the generalizations about the spelling system that can provide them with useful strategies. These people need to challenge a second myth:

There is no logic to English spelling, so why even try?

This myth is reinforced when people point out different ways of spelling the same sound, and spellings that are irregular. Some older students who are chronically poor spellers give up completely, and, in extreme cases, revert to writing strings of random letters; they believe they have no chance of ever spelling correctly, no matter what they try. *What students need to learn is that there are only a limited number of alternatives for spelling a word, not an infinite number of possibilities.* It is important that all students come to understand that the English system of spelling is basically logical, having rational and historical explanations for its differing patterns. This understanding can help dispel a third myth:

Learning to spell is a rote-memory process.

This myth has been perpetuated by many spelling texts and much spelling instruction. Such texts have often been based on the 3 000 most common words, which students were asked to memorize through weekly lists. Often, the words on the lists had no spelling link with one another; the lessons and activities provided activities designed to help memorization. Those students who could memorize words for a test often misspelled these same words in their writing.

Contemporary researchers have redefined spelling, not as a low-level, rote-memorization task, but instead as a high-level cognitive skill. This means that spelling and thinking go hand in hand. To be able to spell, you have to know a great deal about the English language, and be able to apply this knowledge to the construction of words.

If you are a poor speller, you are a poor writer.

Because society puts a high premium on standard spelling, many poor spellers have drawn the conclusion that spelling is the major skill in writing. As a consequence, they believe themselves to be poor writers. Of course, if we want to make a good impression, we want our spelling to be perfect before our writing goes on public view. This is the purpose of proofreading and copy editing. It is important, though, not to confuse spelling and composition. Composition is the creation of writing, involving having something to say, someone to say it to, and the language with which to say it. This must be done first, before there is any need for spelling.

Being a poor speller does not detract from the quality of a person's ideas or the flow of language. The only real spelling requirement for early drafts is that the writer can read back what has been written. The greatest tragedy of spelling occurs when it presents a barrier to writing. While we recognize the importance of spelling, we need to put it in perspective and understand where it fits in the writing process.

8

There are right and wrong ways to spell.

Most of us have at some time been surprised, not to mention horrified, to discover that there are alternate ways to spell words — that there isn't always one right way. People are often bothered by regional and national differences in spelling, believing that there is "our way and the wrong way".

The truth is that spelling is something we made up when we started to keep records. The concept of standard spelling is a relatively new one. Standard spelling is a consensus, not a rule, and is constantly evolving. At any one time, many words are in a process of change, some people using the old way, some adopting the new. Dictionaries recognize this and list the alternatives that are in use. We should not be smug about right and wrong in spelling.

It is not necessary to teach spelling.

The failure of some past methods of spelling instruction has lead some teachers to believe that spelling instruction is a waste of time. Certainly, our students should not be spending time on repetitive rote-memory tasks in preparation for a weekly test, but there are many spelling concepts which can be learned, and which can form the basis of creative instruction. What we need is a new understanding of what the skills of spelling are. If we couple this understanding with our knowledge of how language is learned and practised, then we can help our students to be better spellers.

The Chauvinism of Spelling

Both of us grew up in Britain where the Oxford English Dictionary is the guardian of "truth" about spelling. There, American spelling is considered a bastardization of the "right" way. In the United States, spelling has certainly undergone more changes, some evolutionary, others deliberate and revolutionary. Now we live in Canada, a country of a certain spelling schizophrenia. Some words are spelled the English way, some the American way. As if this were not confusing enough, different parts of the country favour (or favor) different spellings. Even publishers of books and newspapers within the same city may use different spelling guides. If you use an English or an American dictionary you know what you are getting, however, with a Canadian dictionary you take your chances. How is it possible to know what is right? Which version of spelling should we be teaching?

Spelling, like all forms of language, is relative to the user and to the situation. Most of us read books published in all parts of the English-speaking world. When our students read widely, they will notice differences in spellings. They should be encouraged to see this as an example of the flexibility and diversity of language customs, rather than as a problem. Even young children readily learn that they must use different language in different situations: their playground language is not the same as their classroom language, and they know which words they must not say when an adult is listening. Teenagers develop entirely new dialects and vocabularies that change so rapidly many adults feel they cannot communicate with them.

Regional and national dialects used to be considered a problem, something to be eradicated so that everyone would use the same standard speech. In 19th-century England, and well into the 20th century, using the standard dialect was one way of moving up in society, showing that you belonged to the educated classes. Many classrooms today bring together children and adults with vastly different dialects of English, and our attitudes have changed. Now we do our best to have children value and maintain their native speech while being aware of, and able to operate in, standard English. Rather than changing their dialect, we add to it another.

(There is always the question of what is standard English. It is certainly not the same in Cheltenham, Chiliwak, and Chatanooga. Isn't it always the other person who has the dialect? One definition is that standard English is the dialect used by the dominant professional class of the region in which you happen to live. It is often exemplified by news readers on your local television station. Standard English is also relative.)

We need to teach our students that language and spelling vary according to region and nationality. We can then give them options to use when they are making spelling decisions. There are two choices:

1. *Pick a dictionary and stick with it.*
If you live in Chatanooga and you decide the Oxford English

Dictionary is for you, people can say you are quaint and old-fashioned, but they cannot say you are wrong. The sensible choice, however, is to discover the consensus according to where you live and go with the majority.

2. *Vary your spelling according to your audience.*
This is difficult because most of us are very protective of our own spelling customs and believe that our way is the right way. The sophisticated speller, however, knows that spelling is for the reader, not for the writer. You might use English or American spelling according to what you would expect your reader to use. If your reader is Canadian, good luck!

The History of Spelling

You have probably heard that Shakespeare spelt his name at least seven different ways. Perhaps you feel you too would like to have the option of spelling words any way you like. You might still be able to do that today, except for the influence of three men: William Caxton, Samuel Johnston, and Noah Webster. They began the process of formalizing and standardizing written English, first through the invention of the printing press, and later through the creation of dictionaries.

The Printing Press

Until the late Middle Ages, books were rare and had to be copied by hand. The only book most people saw was the Bible, chained in the church. Few people ever saw the printed word — there were no spelling problems. Then, in 1476, the printing press was invented. For the first time in history, people had access to standardized spelling, that is, the spelling chosen by William Caxton, the first printer of the English language. Because Caxton worked in London, he made an arbitrary decision to print the variety of English spoken in London at that time.

There are many spellings Caxton used that we would not employ today, for example:

langage for language   *frenshe* for french
certaynly for certainly   *sayd* for said
englysshe for English   *sayled* for sailed

Because of the limitations of the printing press, Caxton made some practical changes, for example, he changed the "u" to "o" in *come, wonder,* and *love* because his press would not print a good, clean "u".

Although the printing press brought about some standardization of spelling, the idea of Standard English was still very much in its infancy. Other printers established businesses and used different varieties of spoken and written English. Books published in the 16th century reflect the language of their publishers and the regions in which they lived and worked. However, by the time the 1611 version of the Bible was published, the words were much closer to today's spelling, although you can still see the influence of Chaucer's time in words such as these:

shepheard for shepherd
greene for green
walke for walk
oyle for oil
cuppe for cup
shadowe for shadow.

This may be because Caxton had been the first to print Chaucer's works.

The Dictionary

In 1604, a man called Robert Cawdray produced a dictionary of 120 pages called, "A Table Alphabeticall", which he wrote for "Ladies. . .or any other unskilfull persons"!

Samuel Johnson published his dictionary in 1755. It was produced in nine years by Johnson and six assistants working like Bob Cratchet in a garret. In the dictionary, he defined 40 000 words, along with analogies and quotations. Although it was noted for its scholarship and the detail and accuracy of the definitions, this dictionary is probably just as memorable for the sparkle of Johnson's wit:

Pension An allowance made to anyone without an equivalent. In England it is generally understood to mean pay given to a state hireling for treason to his country.

> *Oats*   A grain, which in England is generally given to horses, but in Scotland supports the people.*

It was Johnson's opinion that English spelling tended to favour meaning over sound, and in most cases he made an attempt to spell homophones (bare, bear) differently. However, he did list *flower* with two meanings — "blossom" and "meal".

One of the reasons Dr. Johnson wrote a dictionary was his strong wish that future generations would be able to read Shakespeare's writings, that they would not be lost because of a spelling system which did not reflect changes in pronunciation. His wish came true.

For the new middle class which arose during the industrial revolution, the dictionary was a way to improve one's station in life. Dialect became not only an indication of where one lived, but a mark of social class. For the social climber of Victorian England, speaking and writing "the Queen's English" conferred respectability and a sense of belonging. In the preface to Pygmalion, George Bernard Shaw remarked that "it is impossible for an Englishman to open his mouth without making some other Englishman despise him".

On the other side of the Atlantic, in 1828, Noah Webster compiled the first dictionary of American English, one-third larger than Dr. Johnson's, which set the spelling standard for English-speaking Americans. He also made some arbitrary decisions to change some of the spellings. Examples of his spelling reforms included the following:

color for colour   *defense* for defence
wagon for waggon   *music* for musick
robin for robbin   *tire* for tyre

Although Webster was trying to simplify spelling, he was responsible for creating some new problems. In English spelling, there is a standard pattern that in a word of more than one syllable, when a consonant follows a short vowel, the consonant is doubled, as in *little, Mummy, Daddy, dinner, happy, rabbit, yellow, sunny, letter,* and so on. In his effort to simplify spelling, Webster created two new exceptions: *wagon* and *robin*. He went on to wage a

---

* To which Boswell replied: "Which is why England is famous for its horses, and Scotland for its men."

13

one-man crusade to change spelling. Webster would visit printers with his new spellings written on cards, asking them to please, in future, spell the words his way.

Today, spelling is considered correct or incorrect based on arbitrary and sometimes illogical decisions made by one printer and two writers of dictionaries.

How Language Changes

Although dictionaries standardized spelling, the English language is far from static. Johnson included 40 000 words in his dictionary; Shakespeare used 30 000 words in his writing. In comparison, an educated person today would be unlikely to use a vocabulary of more than 15 000 words. It seems apt that Shakespeare added the word "multitudinous" to our vocabulary.* Today, when a new word is created, there is an outcry in the press about the corruption of the language.

Lewis Carroll began the creation of portmanteau words — words which have two meanings packed into one, such as chortle, a combination of "chuckle" and "snort". Portmanteau words are extremely popular today:

bit (binary + digit = computer term)
brunch (breakfast + lunch)
motel (motor + hotel)
transistor (transfer + resistor)

As well as blending words together to create new words, we sometimes clip words, dropping the longer form and using the shorter form. Examples include:

wig from periwig
cello from violoncello
taxi from taxicab

We also create new words by changing nouns into verbs:

breakfast to breakfasted
golf to golfed
bus to bussed*

---

* He also added *dislocate, obscene, critical, emphasis, initiate, modest, horrid, vast, submerged, assassination,* and many more.

* And the writing teacher's favourite: *conferenced.* We thought the verb was "to confer".

14

or verbs into nouns:

to break down into *breakdown*
to fall out into *fall-out*
to hold up into *hold-up*

As well as changing the shape and function of words over the years, we have in some cases changed their meaning. Sometimes we narrow the meaning of a word. Until the 16th century, the word *deer* meant any kind of animal, and was not limited to a particular type of hoofed animal. This gives new significance to the death penalty imposed on peasants for killing the King's deer — it meant they could die for any kind of poaching. Sometimes we widen the meaning. *Board* was once limited to meaning "a piece of timber", lacking the range of meanings it has today:

meals served in exchange for payment or services
the distance sailed by a ship on one tack
the wall surrounding the ice in hockey
the backboard behind the basket in basketball,

not to mention *boarder, surfboard, baseboard, boardwalk,* and the *Board of Education.*

Another way we change words is by combining two separate words into one — compounding words:

searchlight	snowman
overkill	splashdown
highway	blackbird
breakfast	hotplate

Sometimes words change in meaning because of incorrect usage. The word *apron* used to be spelled "napron". Because people constantly heard "a napron", the spelling changed.

North Americans have recently changed the meaning of *momentarily*. It is formed from the adjective, *momentary*, meaning fleeting or brief. The 1987 Webster's dictionary defines *momentarily* as "lasting for a moment", but it is almost universally used to mean "in a moment". This likely came about because of a desire to sound more literate by using a long word instead of a short one. We still worry when we are told the airplane will be landing momentarily!

It will be interesting to note how long it takes for this change in meaning to be reflected in the dictionary. A dictionary, after all, does not *pre*scribe as much as *de*scribe language as it is used.

This explains why for many words there are two or more acceptable spellings. If enough people use a word incorrectly, either in its spelling or in its meaning, for a long enough period, the incorrect spelling eventually becomes legitimate. You may like to become a kind of spelling anthropologist, and study spelling in change. We have noticed, for example, that the "gue" ending is in the process of disappearing. We often see the words *catalog*, *monolog*, *dialog*, and *epilog*, and our Webster's gives these as alternate spellings. (It does not, however, give any alternate spelling for *synagogue*.) How long will it be before "gue" becomes the alternate? How long before "ue" disappears?

The English language is constantly growing, changing, and becoming more complex. Yet for over 150 years, the spelling of most words has remained the same. The pronunciation of many words has strayed further and further from their original link to sound — the "w" in *two* and the "b" in *tomb* used to be pronounced, but are now silent.* Consequently, the more we know about the origins and evolution of our language, the more chance we have of figuring out how our spelling system works, and how we can master it.

Attempts to Simplify Spelling

Attempts to simplify spelling go back as far as the Middle Ages. In the 15th century, a monk named Ormin tried to make spelling more closely reflect pronunciation. In the 16th century, a Cambridge professor, Sir John Cheke, tried to get rid of silent letters. In the 17th century, another Cambridge master and later bishop, proposed an international phonetic alphabet. In the 18th century, Benjamin Franklin published a paper called, "A Scheme For a New Alphabet and a Reformed Mode of Spelling". At least part of his purpose was to reinforce the concept of an independent America through independence in language. His ideas were not widely accepted, but he was responsible for these spellings: *honor*, *theater*, *plow*, and *curb*. Franklin devised another phonetic alphabet, but he did not publish it, claiming he was too old for a crusade. He was a realist; none of the earlier attempts to simplify spelling had had any measure of success. In the 19th century, Charles Darwin, who we thought understood the laws of

---

* The "w" in *two* is still pronounced in Scotland, as is the "h" in *where*.

natural selection, became associated, along with Alfred, Lord Tennyson, with the British Spelling Reform Association.

In 20th-century England, the British Simplified Spelling Society tried, without success, to get government support for spelling reforms. George Bernard Shaw advocated simplified spelling, leaving part of his fortune for this purpose. In America, Andrew Carnegie financed the Simplified Spelling Board, which proposed three hundred new spellings. Theodore Roosevelt endorsed some of these, and ordered their use in the Government Printing Office. When Roosevelt was defeated by Taft, *The New York Sun* announced the event with a one-word headline: *THRU*.

Noah Webster was at first conservative about spelling, opposing any changes. Later, he did try some simplification, publishing words like *thum, iland, hed, giv, bilt, iz, mashine, yeer*, and *wimmen*. These were retracted in later versions. He was successful in introducing the following: *physic(k), center, theater, honor, favor, traveled, check, mask*, and *defense*.

Despite many attempts, often by well-known and influential people, simplified spelling has never been widely accepted. One problem is that once the spelling of a word has changed, it loses its etymology, and hence, its reason for existence. Spelling has as much to do with meaning as with sound. Phonetic spelling would destroy meaning links between words, such as *mnemonic* and *amnesia, sign* and *signature*. Dialect is another complication.

Perhaps the most serious problem is that people have never been able to agree on which changes are desirable — or even whether change is necessary. After all, who decides? Most prefer that evolution make the decisions for us. There may also be an element of guilt, a feeling that we *ought* to be able to spell, and that making it easier is somehow giving in.

Or do we just like our spelling system the way it is?

The Logic of Spelling

We tend to think of English as a non-phonetic language, composed of totally illogical spellings and pronunciations. Because there are so many different ways to represent the sounds of the language, we may regard spelling as difficult and unpredictable.

In fact, our spelling system is not totally random. We do not have to rely only on memory. A good speller is not a person who has successfully memorized the most words, but rather someone who knows ways to figure out the logic of words and can construct them as needed. Spelling is problem-solving with letters, sounds, patterns, and meanings.

In a way, spelling is rather like trying to find your way around a strange city with the help of a road map. If you know how maps work, and can follow a few basic principles, you can not only find your way, but feel in control of the situation. Even if you get lost once in a while, you can get back on track.

There are three major principles you have to understand in order to use the road map of spelling:

the pattern by sound or alphabetic principle
the pattern by function principle
the pattern by meaning principle

Pattern By Sound

One of the problems with spelling is that there are only twenty six letters in the alphabet, but more than forty sounds in spoken English. If we were inventing a language from scratch, we would likely have a symbol for every sound. (Of course, to do this we would have to eliminate dialect: in the south of England, *bath* and *hearth* rhyme; in the north they do not.) Another problem is that we often spell the same sound in different ways, such as the "f" sound in *far*, *phone*, and *laugh*, and the "u" sound in *nut*, *tough*, *done*, and *blood*.

Nevertheless, many of the sounds in words do correspond to letters or groups of letters. The sound-symbol relationships are predictable for the most part, and follow known patterns. Children begin to spell by using their knowledge of the names of letters, and what they hear when they make sounds in the mouth:

are is written as "r"; *you* as "u"
gate is written as "gat", because they hear "a" in the middle
pin is written as "pen" because short "i" sounds most like the letter "e"
drum is written as "jrum", because they hear "j" at the beginning
laugh is written "laf", because they hear only one sound at the end of the word

When young students write, they concentrate on representing the sounds themselves, thus adhering to the alphabetic principle.

As they become more knowledgeable about words, they are reassured to discover that there are patterns in spelling:

• Most consonant sounds are represented by the letter you expect:

If it sounds like "t", it probably is "t".

• In many words the sound-symbol relationship is highly predictable:

dad, remember, prehistoric.

• There are many clusters of words which share the same sound-symbol pattern:

gate, state, relate, berate, stagnate, delegate
seat, cheat, neat, treat, beater, defeat, creature.

• There are patterns related to the sequence of letters in a word:

we always use "qu" for a "kw" sound at the beginning of words.

• Some sounds are represented by two letters:

shape, shop, smash
chin, check, church.

This alphabetic principle allows us to make a reasonable attempt at spelling most words. All we need to know is which combinations of letters are probable, which are possible, which are improbable, and which are impossible.*

Pattern By Function

Many patterns relate to how a word is used — the function it serves in a sentence. This is how it works:

If you were to rely on sound only, you would spell the past tense of *walked, waited,* and *warned* as "walkt", "waitid", and "warnd".

We know this is not right because "ed" is a past tense marker: the sound may change, but the spelling does not.* Our spelling

---

* For more about probables, possibles, improbables, and impossibles, see p. 23.

* There are only a few exceptions to the "ed" rule, for example, *spelt, blest, dwelt, burnt.*

system signals the past tense graphically. This pattern is not only logical, it is helpful in reading. It can also be a helpful pattern in spelling. If you can apply it correctly to one word, then you can apply it to them all.

Other examples of pattern by function are plurals, possessives, and contractions. Once you know the pattern, you can apply it in new situations.

Some spelling patterns are structural markers; the presence of one or more letters affects the pronunciation of others, for example, *hop* and *hope*, *hoping* and *hopping*, and *courageous* (soft "g").

We know that young children are learning function patterns in speech when they say words like *wented* and *goed*. This tells us that they have made a generalization about the structure of past tense verbs, and can apply this knowledge in new situations. They will make similar generalizations about usage patterns when they are learning to spell.

Pattern By Meaning

Often the meaning of a word helps us with the spelling. Meaning is linked to derivation, the use of affixes to build words from a root or base, often with a change in the part of speech:

predict	prediction	contradiction	interdiction
like	likely	unlikely	likelihood

Even when pronunciation changes, the spelling does not:

please	pleasant
revise	revision
medicine	medical
nation	national

Even when emphasis changes, the spelling does not:

derive	derivation

Knowing that words are derived from the same base helps us put in letters we would otherwise omit:

autumn	autumnal
condemn	condemnation
solemn	solemnity
mnemonic	amnesia
sign	signal

design   designate
muscle   muscular

Knowing how to add a prefix can help us avoid some of the most misspelled words:

mis spell
de siccate

As we build a knowledge of common prefixes, suffixes and root words, we add to the information we can call on to help us spell.

Following the Road Map

Using these three kinds of information in combination helps us to create words we need to spell. Learning to spell is not just a matter of memorizing words. None of us learned all the words we can spell by memorization. We must keep the number of words we have to memorize as low as possible.

Spelling is a skill of constructing words.

Once we know the three main roads of spelling, more experience with language will help us recognize the dead-end streets and the exceptions to predictable patterns. Misreading the map is not a major problem because we can monitor our progress, ask directions, retrace our steps, self-correct, and start again.

If students understand how the spelling system works, they feel they have some control over it. A feeling of control can enable one to manipulate language with a reasonable chance of using it accurately. Spelling will no longer be a maze students wander blindly through, but a series of problems they can solve with strategies.

2. How Spelling Is Learned

What Good Spellers Don't Know They Know

You may have seen the following phonic joke written by George Bernard Shaw:

What is this word?

ghoti

Here are the phonic rules for you to sound it out:

"gh" as in *rough*
"o" as in *women*
"ti" as in *nation*

Isn't it strange how difficult sounding out is when you don't know the word?

The really interesting point, though, is the word *ghoti*. We all know that this could not possibly be an English word because of its appearance. The estimated number of words in the English language is about two million, depending on how many scientific words and derivations you decide to include. In our lives, we will meet only a fraction of these words. A quick browse through a medium-sized dictionary reveals hundreds of words we have never seen. How do we know, then, that *ghoti* could not be an English word?

Well, we know that "gh" does not make the sound of "f" at the beginnings of words. It sometimes does in the middle or at the end, but **never** at the beginning. None of us learned this in school. Even the most dedicated and thorough of phonics teachers did not think of this rule, yet we all know it. This rule is one of the hundreds of generalizations we have made about language through our reading and writing. Most of the time we are not aware of it, but it is this kind of intrinsic knowledge about how words are supposed to look — what is possible and what is impossible — that enables us to spell.

A good speller is a person who has a sense of what is probable, what is possible, what is improbable, and what is impossible in English spelling. This is how we make predictions about how words are likely to be spelled.* There are so many generalizations that we could not attempt to teach them all, even if we could work out what they are. What we can do is help our students increase their awareness and make their own generalizations by doing the following:

- Have them read, read, read. Spelling patterns are largely visual, and we want students to see the patterns of words over and over again.
- Help them to express themselves through oral language. Enunciation and pronunciation are also important to spelling. An awareness of correct pronunciation can prevent errors in words like *February* and *government*.
- Have students write in different modes and for different purposes and audiences. In this way, they will practise word construction.
- Take every opportunity to teach students to look for patterns and similarities in words. Though we cannot teach all the patterns, we can teach the *concept* that patterns are there to be discovered.
- Engage students' interest in words and language. The more they question and investigate, the more they will learn about the possibles, the probables, the improbables, and the impossibles of spelling.

The word in the puzzle is *fish*.

---

* We first heard this concept of a sliding scale from probability to impossibility when talking in the early 1980s with a former colleague, Chris Worsnop. He says he got it from his reading of Aristotle's *Poetics*. Worsnop believed then, and still does, that the errors people make in spelling can be assessed according to this scale, and would like to use the concept in a research project to establish a spelling equivalent to the Reading Miscue Inventory.

How We Have Taught Spelling in the Past

The Practical Speller, published by Gage and Company in 1881, bemoans in its preface the demise of the old-fashioned Spelling Book, stating that, "They took our bread and have given in return but a stone. The bread even though a little stale was much more wholesome than the stone." It seems spelling was in poor shape then: ". . . pupils are turned loose on society to shock it by their bad spelling, and disgrace the schools which they attended, and in which they should have been taught". In a Civil Service Exam of the time in England, "no less than 1 861 out of 1 972 failures were caused by spelling."

The Practical Speller's answer to this is a book of themed word lists and passages for dictation. There is no attempt to group together words with common spelling patterns. There are no lesson plans or strategies, just the lists. The teaching emphasis is on articulation and seeing with precision: the implication is clear that correct teaching is the answer to all problems. Words and dictations are to be written on the slates to imprint the look of the word on the students' minds. Some of the suggested strategies seem more modern. As examples, there is space for the students to make their own word lists, and the importance of reading is emphasized, along with the statement, "It is desirable that spelling should be taught to a considerable extent by means of *composition*, in order to give the pupils practice in spelling the words in their *own* vocabularies."

This memorization of word lists has been the common pattern for most spelling instruction in the past. Many of us remember the weekly (or weakly) spelling bees that were held, in which we were forced to display our knowledge, or lack thereof, before our classmates. We were placed in a situation of high anxiety and embarrassment that made the task difficult, even for good spellers. It is unlikely that this taught us much about spelling: we learned nothing new as we paraded only existent knowledge. Moreover, as spelling is primarily a visual skill, and we never got to see the words, important information about spelling patterns had no chance to become imprinted on our minds.

As we grew older, learning to spell was a matter of correcting all the errors we made in our writing. Occasionally, we had to write the words three times at the bottom, as a way of aiding our memories. The teacher did all the proofreading, marking errors with a "sp" in the margin, and writing comments about "careless mistakes". Of course, this was always single-draft writing, in which we were supposed to make everything come out perfect the first time.

Newer methods of instruction recognise the visual nature of spelling by teaching study steps such as the following: look at the word, picture it in your mind, look away and write the word, look back and check. If a word cannot be linked into a pattern, and rote memorization is the only strategy available, this may help in the short term. However, this kind of rote-memory work is only useful if the word is then used frequently enough for it to pass into long-term memory. Frequent usage is more likely to bring about learning than the study steps. One dangerous side-effect of this study-step method is that it focuses attention on learning one word at a time, rather than on making spelling links. If the study-step method is used frequently, it may teach students that memorization is the only way to learn to spell.

We have sometimes tried to make sense of spelling by grouping together words that are constructed in similar ways, to make "word families". A word family might be composed of rhyming words, words with the same prefix or suffix, past-tense verbs sharing the same ending, words from the same Latin or Greek root, or words which use the same group of letters, like "tch". This makes good spelling sense, because if you know one word in the "family", you have a good chance of being able to spell the others as well. However, lists in spelling texts are commonly based not on word families, but on lists of high-frequency words. In the list, linked words are often buried among unrelated words.

Sometimes word lists seem to be designed to confuse the learner. In a recently-published speller, one lesson objective is to teach that the sound /e/ can be spelled "ee", "ea", and "ie". If this isn't confusing enough, the word list also includes the following: *rest*, *friend*, *they*, and *yard*.

Because we recognise the importance of writing in creating the purpose for spelling, and the place of spelling as part of the writing process, many teachers have advocated having students create their own spelling lists with words taken from their own writing. Of course, students need to spell the words they use often in their writing; if they are not using the words, why do they need to learn them? But students will only learn to make spelling generalizations if they deal with words in *spelling contexts*

— groups of words which share a spelling pattern. When words are selected from a student's writing, they must be placed in their spelling contexts so that the student can make the necessary spelling links. Having students use "study steps" on words they have chosen from their writing is not likely to lead to lasting spelling learning. It results only in another list of unconnected words to be memorized.

There is another school of thought that says plenty of reading and writing are all you need to learn how to spell. If this were true, all prolific readers and writers would be good spellers. This is not the case. It is possible to be a good reader but a poor speller and vice versa. While reading and writing provide information about words, a purpose for understanding how they work, and a medium for using them, they are not enough for many people to become good spellers. Fluent readers look at very little of the visual information on the page; this explains why many good readers and spellers cannot proofread well. Even beginning readers use context clues which enable them to figure out words and phrases without looking at all the letters or the syllables. Often, the details of words are overlooked.

There is clearly a need for a new kind of spelling instruction, one that raises students' awareness about language and its patterns, and focuses on word construction rather than word memorization.

The Spelling/Writing Connection

As soon as students begin to write, they become aware of the need for spelling. Memorizing a map of a city you have no intention of visiting would be an impossible task, not to mention an enormous waste of time. Writing gives spelling meaning.

Writing not only provides the medium for using spelling, but also a context for learning to spell. It is not enough just to write. It is of little importance if we make spelling errors on our shopping list; the important thing is whether we can read it when we get to the store. To provide motivation for correct spelling, the writing must be intended for another to read. If the spelling is poor, we will make a bad impression, and may fail to communicate our true meaning. No one wants to look silly in print. For writing to be a significant factor in learning to spell, the writer must be writing for a real audience. Without audience, there is no need for standard spelling.

The idea of teaching spelling through the students' writing has given rise to a number of misconceptions. It is a good idea to give the students words they need for writing in progress: we know that if they need the words, they are more likely to learn them. However, picking out words and using them to make a personal spelling list once again reduces spelling to a rote-memory skill. We know that rote learning is the hardest way to learn, is typically short-lived, and therefore cannot be viewed as a productive strategy. Lists of "theme words" can provide a ready reference for the spellings of words and encourage students to use them, but these lists will not often provide a spelling context to help the students learn the words.

Spelling errors in writing may be treated in two ways. One is a focus on proofreading and correcting, which involves identifying words that are misspelled and replacing them with the standard spellings. The second is a focus on spelling instruction, which involves helping the student to form links between words, make new generalizations about spellings, and connect the words in some way with the student's existent spelling knowledge. This may mean setting the word in a sound-based or word-family context with other words that look and sound the same. It may be teaching a pattern by function, such as an "ed" ending or a contraction. It may be providing a meaning link, such as *medicine* and *medical*. For long-term spelling learning to occur, the word taken from the writing must be placed in a spelling context.

We must ensure that spelling never interferes with composition. This is why spelling should not be taught while the student is engaged in writing a first draft. By drawing the student's attention to spelling at inappropriate stages of the writing, we work against what we are trying to teach about the writing process. One thing our students must know is that during the writing of a first draft the idea is to focus primarily on content. When we respond to the student, either through written comments or during a conference, we are entitled to comment only on the focus of the student. If this was content, then that is what we evaluate and talk about. If we start commenting on spelling at this stage, even to praise, then the student will learn that spelling is an important factor in first-draft writing, and must therefore be a focus at that time. This is not productive in the process of writing successfully, nor is it productive in the teaching of spelling. There is a time in the writing process when spelling will be a major focus. At this stage, we may evaluate the student's spelling, talk about it, teach about it, and expect the student's full attention. It is important to give a student one aspect to focus on at a time.

Developmental Learning

The way children learn to spell is much like the way they learned to talk. They start by imitating what they see the people around them doing, gradually coming closer to using standard forms.

When young children are learning to spell, they tend to show their learning by a particular sequence. This is what it looks like:

Example # 1

• They scribble in wavy, horizontal lines in an imitation of writing.

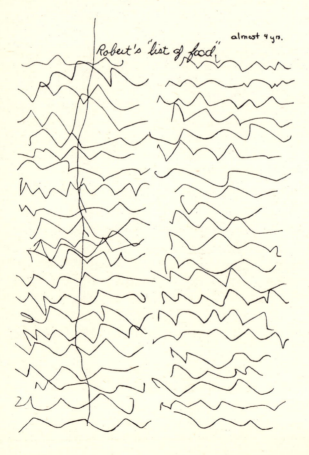

Robert's "list of food"   almost 4 yrs.

Example #2

- They print a series of random letters.

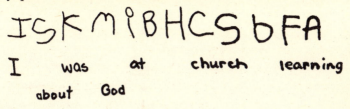

I was at church learning about God

Example #3

- They print one consonant to represent each word. It is usually the first sound of the word:

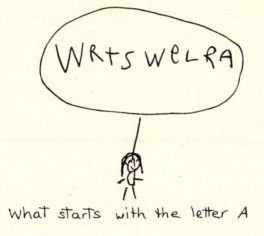

What starts with the letter A

Example #4

- They begin to print a final letter, as well as an initial letter. At this point, they begin to put spaces between the words.

When this thing happened it was like I fell down on the side walk

29

Example #5

• All syllables and sounds in words are represented by letters.

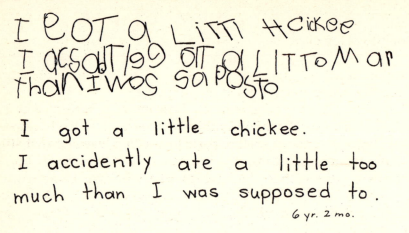

I got a little chickee.
I accidently ate a little too
much than I was supposed to.

6 yr. 2 mo.

The students now know enough about how spelling works to begin to build a repertoire of spelling patterns, and add to their store of sight words.

This experience of building words on the basis of letter sounds teaches students the alphabetic principle, one of the three cueing systems of spelling. It also teaches the basic spelling concept: words are not memorized but constructed using the best available information.

When the students have reached a stage where they are close to standard spelling, they can begin to learn the many patterns and generalizations which enable us to be good spellers. Because there are so many patterns to learn, it will take a number of years before they have enough experience and knowledge to be accurate spellers. While they are learning, we must accept that there is much young students have not had a chance to learn, and help them keep the faith that eventually they will become spellers.

Learning Through Interaction

Learning to spell, like learning anything else, is a dynamic and concrete process, not a passive and abstract one. We learn by active involvement, not by being told. Therefore, it is vital that the students interact with the language system, with one another, and according to their individual learning styles.

Interaction with the Language System

We all learned to speak by *using* language, not by being taught *about* language. As small children, we were largely unaware that we were learning language; it was an accident, a by-product of our involvement in life. As we experienced new situations, were surrounded by role-models, and received help at the moment we needed it, we gradually extended and refined our knowledge and became proficient users of language.

Children learn to spell in much the same way. Writing creates a need for spelling, while reading provides models of what spelling looks like. It is therefore basic to spelling learning that students engage in reading and writing as much as possible. Once the need is there, then we can teach them when and how to focus on spelling. If we provide help as and when it is needed, students will be able to build up their knowledge of how language and spelling work.

A classroom must provide many opportunities for students to talk, read, and write. Sometimes activities will be initiated and structured by the teacher; at other times students will follow their own interests. Whatever the spelling task, the teacher can provide models, supply information, and allow plenty of time for experimentation and practice.

Interaction with One Another

We know that talking and writing are not just ways of showing what we know. They are also important ways of learning new information and concepts.

Students may interact with a partner, a small group, the teacher, or another adult. This interaction can have a spelling focus:

- working collectively to build word-family lists
- proofreading each other's writing
- researching information about words
- sharing information about words
- asking for help
- talking about spelling problems, and spelling learning
- playing word games, and solving puzzles.

Collaborating in this way can help students reflect on their learning, and increase awareness of spelling concepts. They may also learn that others share the same difficulties and frustrations, that they are not alone, and that even their teacher has spelling problems.

Interaction According to Learning Style

Although spelling is a highly visual skill, not all people learn best in a visual mode. Some are auditory learners, while others are kinesthetic, or tactile learners. Each of us learns in our own way. Most of us do not fall exclusively into one group; we may benefit from experience with all three kinds of learning. Students should therefore have opportunities for different modes of interaction to:

• record words, in order to note configurations and patterns
• hear words, generate words orally, listen for patterns
• talk about words, patterns, and generalizations
• handle and feel letters and words in different sizes and textures
• dictate words for a visual learner to write
• record words in a variety of ways, for example, using chart paper and markers, keyboard, plasticine, and a sand table
• form words with letter cards
• play word games
• categorize and classify words.

When students work in a variety of groupings, different learning styles will usually be represented. The students can then be exposed to different kinds of thinking and methods of learning.

How to Help Spelling Learning

• Publish and display student writing to create a need for standard spelling.
• Focus on spelling only at appropriate times during the writing process.
• Teach students that spelling is a thinking activity, and not a memory activity.
• Teach students when, where, and why spelling matters — and when it is less important.
• Encourage any attempt students make to spell.
• Help students move to the next stage of developmental spelling.
• Provide information about words when students need it.

- Point out interesting facts about links between words, word origins, and so on.
- Help students to link words into "word families" which have the same spelling pattern.
- Teach one spelling concept or pattern at a time.
- Give regular instruction in spelling concepts, in the patterns of words, and the construction of words.
- Teach spelling by using groups of words that share a spelling pattern.
- Encourage games and puzzles that involve words.
- Encourage students to share strategies that help them to spell.
- Teach proofreading for specific things, such as plurals.
- Teach students about the function of spelling patterns. As an example, an "er" ending often indicates a person who does something (baker, teacher).
- Nurture a growing awareness of word meanings, origins, and derivations.
- Demonstrate and encourage the use of reference materials.
- Assess spelling proficiency in real writing contexts, and at final draft stage.
- Form your expectations according to what each student knows and is capable of learning, not according to standardized norms. Help the students to be equally realistic about their own progress.
- Build a record of what the students know about spelling, rather than what they don't know. Share this with the students.
- Respect each student's right to privacy and anonymity.
- Show the students how their knowledge about spelling is growing.
- Inform parents about your spelling program, and help them to learn how spelling learning works.

How to Hinder Spelling Learning

- Expect to see accurate spelling at early stages in learning.
- Impress on students that spelling is of primary importance in writing.
- Make spelling instruction a major part of the writing program.
- Teach students that all words have to be memorized.
- Expect students to look up all their errors in the dictionary.
- Require corrected spelling in every piece of student writing.

- Teach spelling by using lists of words which do not share a spelling pattern or generalization. (This leaves memorization as the only strategy.)
- Measure spelling proficiency by scores on tests.
- Draw conclusions about spelling ability by evaluating first-draft writing.
- Downgrade student writing because of spelling errors.
- Focus on students' weaknesses.
- Send home lists of words to be memorized.

Seven Keys to Understanding Spelling	
1. Spelling is generated	not dictated.
2. Spelling is integrated	not isolated.
3. Spelling is internalized	not memorized.
4. Good spellers make logical connections	not laborious corrections.
5. Good spelling is the result of informed prediction	not wild guesses.
6. Good spellers know a great deal about language	not just a great deal about phonics.
7. Spelling is an interactive language process	not a set of rules.

Special Help for Poor Spellers

You will have to do a little extra for those students who see themselves as poor spellers, and who subsequently assume they are also poor writers. These students often write very little because they know they will make mistakes. Writing less will not help them in either composing or in spelling. We need to encourage them to write more, not less. Here are some ways you can help such students gain the courage to write:

- These students know they have problems. Place emphasis on what they do well, rather than on what they do poorly.

- Do everything necessary to make them aware that you are interested in what they have to say, rather than in their spelling.
- Reassure them that being poor spellers does not mean they are poor writers. Prove you mean it by focusing on their composition, and not on their spelling. Ignore their spelling for as long as it takes to make these students focus solely on composition.
- At editing and final draft stages, do not overwhelm them with looking things up, correcting words, and recopying. Focus on only one element at a time.
- If a lot of writing leads inevitably to a lot of correcting, these students will not write. To prevent this, provide all the secretarial help they need, whenever they ask for it. This may help reduce anxiety levels, and expand writing abilities and experiences.
- Provide alternate ways for students to have their ideas and compositions preserved: they may tell or tape their stories; they may illustrate their stories and have someone else transcribe their words; they may present reports orally or graphically; they may use a tape-recorder and then transcribe their own words.
- Encourage team-work. In a group, one person can focus on spelling while others focus on ideas and language. This helps to separate composition and transcription in the early stages of writing, as well as in the minds of the students.
- Provide time and help outside regular writing times to help the students work on their weaknesses.
- With the students, set small objectives to give the maximum opportunity for success.
- Poor spellers often omit whole syllables. Teach these students to listen for syllables and try to represent each one in letters. Then teach them that every syllable has a vowel or ''y''. (Knowing where to divide syllables is not necessary; it is enough to know how many there are.)
- Give students time to work on a computer. Composing on a keyboard is particularly useful for poor spellers, as self-correction is easy. Also, their writing will not become public or permanent until they are satisfied that it is ready.
- In extreme cases, do not mention spelling. Refuse to talk about it. Keep this up for as long as it takes to get the students to write.
- Make sure that these students share in the joys and rewards of authorship and audience response. There is no greater motivator for writing and spelling learning.

- Be sure to explain to parents what you are doing and why. Reassure them that you are still teaching the student about spelling but at other times and in other ways. Suggest ways parents can support your efforts at home.*

---

* For more information, see Keeping Parents Informed, p. 98.

3. What to Teach About Spelling

What Spelling is For

Spelling is one of the less interesting and more laborious aspects of writing. It can also be the most noticeable, one that can create a good or bad impression before a reader thinks about what the writer has to say. Therefore, whether we like it or not, spelling is important.

Students will be more apt to spend time and trouble on spelling and other aspects of transcription if they themselves see a real need for it. Here are some things the students need to understand:

- People will form an opinion of you based on the attractiveness and accuracy of your writing. If your spelling is incorrect, you will make a poor impression.
- If your writing is hard to read, others will often give up and not bother to finish reading your piece.
- Punctuation makes things easier to read and understand. Sometimes it can change the meaning of a sentence.
- Poor spelling can be distracting for a reader, and can make a stronger impression than your composition.
- Any kind of "noise" in the message can hinder your meaning. Poor spelling is noise.
- Sometimes a misspelling can change your meaning.

The best way for students to learn these basic truths is to have many different purposes and audiences for their writing. Spelling and neatness are more for the reader than for the writer. Without a reader, they have no purpose.

Teach students that correct spelling and neat, attractive presentation are courtesies to your reader. They are also ways to put on your best face, to make a good impression. It is rather like cleaning house when visitors are expected, or combing your hair before having your photograph taken. There are occasions when we all want to look our best.

When Does Spelling Count?

Students need to know when spelling matters. Those who have difficulty with spelling give themselves away easily. If you have your class write something, and a student asks, ''Does spelling count?'' you know that he or she has a problem. If a writer does not know whether to focus on spelling or content, then the writing cannot be successful. We want our students to put time and effort into spelling when it is called for — we do not want them wasting time on it when it is not appropriate.

> To think spelling always matters is as non-productive as thinking it never matters.

As adults, we know when correctness matters. During a first draft, we usually make an attempt to spell as correctly as possible; we may stop and think about a word or make a second attempt to spell it. However, we will not usually break our train of thought to fetch the dictionary; we are likely to make a note to check on the spelling later. Few bother to recopy writing that no one is going to see. If the shopping list is messy, who cares? However, if the list is for someone else to see, we take time to ensure neatness and correct spelling.

Students need to understand that in a final draft, standard spelling and attractive presentation are important. Up to this stage in the writing process, paying attention to composition, language use, and organization of information are far more important, and should receive the writer's full attention. This is a simple rule that students can learn. They will only learn it, though, if classroom writing follows the rules and customs of the outside world.

- Spelling is never a focus of first-draft writing.
- In personal writing that only the writer will see, spelling is the writer's choice.
- You always have a chance to check your writing before you are to be judged on spelling.
- No one knows, or cares, who helped with spelling, or how many words needed to be corrected.
- Spelling is important in writing that is to go public.

You can teach the place of spelling by practising some of the following guidelines:

- Do not make a final draft the automatic completion of all writing tasks. All writing will not be seen by others.
- Ignore spelling at early stages of writing. Do not mention it, do not give spellings, pretend it does not exist. If students ask about spellings, tell them to do the best they can and that you will help them when the composition is done.
- Do not criticize or congratulate students about spelling, except at the final editing stage. Show that, up to this point, it does not matter.
- Provide opportunities for students to display or publish their writing, so that there is a legitimate reason for accuracy.
- If there is an opportunity to teach a spelling concept through a student's writing, do it only after the content is complete.
- Always expect correct spelling in a final draft. Give praise at this time only.*

It is important to constantly reinforce these truths about spelling. The students need to hear the same message in all subjects, from all teachers, and from their parents. No matter what the task or the topic, spelling is done the same way and for the same reasons.

The Las Vegas Rules of Spelling

English spelling is noted for exceptions to rules. Many of the

---

* You can be more flexible once a student knows the place of spelling, and when and where to focus on it.

rules we learned in school have so many exceptions they cannot be called rules at all. It is often these exceptions that cause spelling problems. When so-called "rules" let students down, they may once again feel they have no strategies for spelling, and subsequently, no control.

A far more reliable system is to follow the Las Vegas Rules and play the odds. To understand playing the odds, consider the spelling of the sound, "shun".

First, we can learn that at the end of a word this sound is **never** spelled "shun". This is useful information, especially for young students who will try to spell it this way.

We have found twelve ways of spelling this sound:

tion	sion	cean	shion	tian	sian
cian	cion	chian	chion	cheon	xion

A poor speller might expect to have a very slim chance of being right — or an eleven out of twelve chance of being wrong. Not so. Look at the odds:

In eight out of nine cases, this sound is spelled "tion".

Here are even better odds. If you hear "a-shun", there are at least 1 200 words with "ation", and only four exceptions!

We found very few examples for some of the possible spellings:

one word ending in "chion"
two words ending in "chian"
two common words ending in "xion" (along with three we have never seen before, much less used)
two words ending in "shion"
two words ending in "cean"
two words ending in "cion"
three words ending in "cheon".

Very few of these are common words. They can almost be ignored.

A Las Vegas Rule for spelling the sound of "shun" therefore would be:

If in doubt, choose "tion".

If you do this, you will be right 88% of the time. You will also know that you have a strategy to use; you will not be helpless.

As for the 12%, you might try to memorize any of the words you think you will use frequently. The list to be memorized will be very small. You can make memorizing easier by considering the following patterns:

• The "cian" ending is used for a kind of job:

dietician musician politician statistician pediatrician
If you know one, then you know them all.

• The "tian" ending is used for a nationality:

Laotian Egyptian Haitian

(You can remember that it is "ian" by making a link with *Canadian*, where the sound tells you there is an "a".)

These "sian" endings for nationalities give themselves away by their hard sound:

Asian Malaysian Indonesian

Again, if you know one, then you know them all. One exception is *Russian*, but you would have to be a creative speller to spell it with "tian". You won't need to worry about *Grecian* — we don't use it much any more, except in an ode by Keats.

• Most words ending in "sion" give themselves away by their hard sound:

evasion lesion division erosion confusion

This is always the case when there is a vowel before the "sion". Also note: *version*, *dispersion* and *aspersion*, which can be pronounced either "shun or "zhun". To make a real "shun" or "sion" sound, the word must fall into one of these patterns:

re**vuls**ion pe**ns**ion se**ss**ion
mansion mission
passion

We are not suggesting that patterns like these be listed and learned. We offer them as examples of the kinds of spelling and meaning links that can be made among words. These types of patterns form part of our intrinsic knowledge about words. Often, we are not aware that we have made a generalization about a spelling pattern, but it is this knowledge that enables us to know which words are spelled in similar ways.

Many people make their own generalizations about words that are spelled in a similar way. Those who don't are the ones most likely to make spelling errors. You can help your students make these kinds of links. Whenever you give a student the spelling of a word, build a list of others which are formed in the same way. Point out what it is that makes them similar. The word lists you build up will show you patterns like these:

rarefy	testify	certify	acidify
putrefy	amplify	beautify	calcify
liquefy	clarify	gratify	horrify
stupefy	dignify	falsify	fortify
	glorify	mummify	mystify
	petrify	qualify	rectify
	signify	specify	terrify

If in doubt, which ending would you pick?

By playing the odds, you can use the Las Vegas Rules of Spelling to reduce your chances of making spelling errors, and to give you more confidence in figuring out words.

Teaching the Las Vegas Rules of Spelling

There are three main principles to the Las Vegas Rules:

always
never
most of the time

Here are some examples of the three principles.

Always

- A "kw" sound is spelled "qu".
  (The only exceptions are found in one or two brand names.)
- "Q" is always followed by "u".
- Every syllable has a vowel or "y".
- Soft "c" and soft "g" are followed by "i", "y", or "e".
  (penicillin, cygnet, censorship; prestigious, gyrate, general)
- When you hear "qu" + short "o", write "qu" + "a".
  (squash, quarrel)
- If a word sounds as if it starts with "f", and it doesn't, it starts with "ph".
- If a word sounds as if it ends with "f", and it doesn't, it ends with "ph", or more rarely, "gh".

42

• Use "dge" after short vowels, and "ge" after long vowels. (fudge, cage)

Most of the Time

• Words do not end in "i". Use "y". The ending "ie" is rare.
  (taxi is short for taxicab, maxi and mini are also abbreviations)
• Occupations end in "er" or "or".
  (not "ar", "ur", "ir", "our". . ." "er" is the most common,
  for example teacher, carpenter; sailor, doctor)*
• Use "le" at the ends of words. It is far more common than "el".
  (fumble, nickel)
• A "k" sound at the beginning of a word is most likely to be
  "c". It is rarely "k", and even more rarely "ch".
  (cactus, kerosene, chorus)
• A "k" sound at the end of a word will not be written "k".
  It will be "ck" or "c".
  (knock, attic)*
• Words ending in "c" will end in "ic" or "iac".
• "ary" or "ery"? A place where something is made ends in "ery".
  (baker-bakery, brewer-brewery)*
• When you hear "chur" at the end of a word, write "ture".
  (picture, nature, creature)
• After a short vowel, put "t" before "ch".
  (dispatch, ketch, pitch, scotch, crutch)
  The only exceptions are these one syllable words: much, such,
  rich, which; and these multi-syllable words: ostrich, duchess,
  sandwich, attach, bachelor.
• "Er", "or", "ar", "ur"? If it is a verb, it will end in "er".
  (deliver, sequester)*

---

* Some modern "or" endings are fashionable but wrong — presentor.
* Note: trek
* note: factory
* Note: favour/favor, savour/ savor

Never

- Never write "shun" at the end of a word.
- No English words end in "j", "v", or "q".*
  (judge, rage, live, toque)
- Never write "kk". Use "ck" instead.
  (rocker)
- There are several other letters we never put in pairs.*

These, and many more that you and your students can discover, are important spelling concepts which students can learn and practise daily as they write. In this way, students can build up a store of useful information to give them strategies for solving future spelling problems.

Were you wondering about the "shun" words we found? Here they are:

stanchion
eustachian, Appalachian
complexion, crucifixion (plus transfixion, fluxion and flexion, although flection is more common)

fashion, cushion
ocean, crustacean
suspicion, coercion
luncheon, truncheon, puncheon

And the four exceptions to the "a-shun" rule:

Dalmatian   Appalachian

crustacean   eustachian

As a child, one of us made bread in a pancheon. We cannot find this word in a dictionary, and do not know how it is spelled. This is our best guess. We invented this spelling by seeing which of the possibilities looked the most likely.* Also, it is probable that *pancheon* is a regional variation of "puncheon", as both words mean a large, earthenware vessel. This is the kind of logic we all use when we come to spell an unfamiliar word. Usually, we have enough knowledge of patterns, origins, and derivations to

---

* Our motorist friends insist they "rev" their engines. We think this is the only exception, presumably derived from "revolution".
* *revved* is the only "vv" word we can find.
* See Visualizing, p. 52

come up with the probable spelling — or at least a possible spelling. We feel certain the spelling "panshun" is impossible.

Handling Homophones

Homophones are words that sound the same but have different spellings and meanings. Here are some examples of words used every day that are frequently misspelled.

where	to	there	here
wear	too	their	hear
ware	two	they're	

We have made the mistake in the past of teaching these words as sets. We have written *where, wear,* and *ware* on the board and said to the students, "never confuse these three words." We have then expected them to memorize the spellings along with the meanings. This method has failed.

In order to determine which spelling to use, students must first place the word in a spelling context. This will give them a pattern they can use — a logical way to figure out the spelling. The homophones listed above are grouped into sound patterns. This is not useful, in fact, it makes spelling more difficult. What makes the words different is not their sound, but their meaning. Therefore, it makes more spelling sense to group them according to meaning:

here	*This gives a group of words*
there	*to do with location.*
where	
somewhere	
everywhere	
nowhere	
whereabouts	

Once you know the location words, you can easily determine that *hear* and *wear* do not belong in this pattern. You may have to stop and think about it, but you will know you are right. ("Ware" is now only used as a suffix, as in *hardware* and *software*, so it falls into a group of its own. If you think of meaning, you will not put *underwear* in this group.) You will also have narrowed down your options for spelling *their* and *they're* from three to two. Once you are keyed in to thinking of meaning, and if you know about contractions, you can distinguish between these two by trying to put *they are* into your sentence. *Their* is one you have to learn in its own group of sight words:

their	his	your
my	her	our

You can put these on a cheat sheet until you can remember them.*

Too is one of the most misspelled words in every year of elementary school. Students probably read or write it every day, and it is taught and corrected repeatedly, yet they do not learn it. The three spellings of this sound can be taught in this way:

First, teach the pattern of the number words:

two
twice
twenty
twins

This will show a reason for the silent "w". Tell the students that in Scotland the "w" is sounded "twa". Find a Scottish person to talk to the students. Have some fun with a Robert Burns poem or twa.* Talk about how language changes over time.

Now you are down to two options instead of three. You can then use a mnemonic trick,* for example:

too many, two "o's".

Or, you can use a pronunciation cue, for example:

Think of the three bears of the fairy tale. Exaggerate the sound, "the porridge was *tooooo* hot; the chair was *tooooo* big".

Even in normal speech, to and too do not usually sound the same:

I am going *to* school. (the "o" is barely sounded)
I was *too* late. (the "o" is longer)

Tell the students to listen for the extra "o".

For homophones such as *right* and *write*, which do not fall into

---

* See Cheat Sheets, p. 80.
* for example, Three craws sat upon a wa'. The second verse begins: Twa craws sat upon a wa'.
* For more about mnemonic devices, see p. 59.

obvious meaning patterns, help the students to make associa-
tions by building word families:

right	sight	light	might
bright	fight	tight	plight

For one-syllable words, this is the most common pattern for this
sound. The students may then have to learn *write* as an exception, and link it with *wrote, written,* and *writing.* One hopes *writing*
is a word with which they will be familiar.

Do not bother with *rite.* It is a word students will not need
for some time. Learning to spell should be kept as simple as possible and confined to concepts and words the students are likely
to use. If you wish, tell them that *rite* is a word, but not one they
need to learn now.

One advantage of drawing students' attention to homophones
and their problems is that they become aware of high-risk words.
The students can look out for them when they are proofreading,
and check that they have used the right spelling.

There are two good principles to remember when teaching
homophones:

1. Group words together because the spelling is similar. Never
   group words because they are different, for example, *here,
   there,* and *where;* never *where, wear,* and *ware.*
2. Teach one homophone at a time along with its group of similar words. Do not try to teach two or three alternate spellings
   at the same time.

Patterns and Generalizations

The more patterns you know and the more able you are to make
generalizations, the better speller you will be. We are not always
aware of it, but we apply our knowledge of patterns constantly
as we write.

Knowing a pattern or word family can be useful to students
as they try to spell. While it is possible and often necessary to
memorize single words, especially those we use frequently, it
can be far more productive to teach spelling patterns that can
be applied to many words.

Many of the generalizations we have made about spelling are
subconscious. Often, we are only aware that some letter combi-

nations look right and others do not. Can you think of a word in which a double vowel is followed by a double consonant?* Probably not. If you tried to put this combination in a word, it would look wrong. This is a generalization you have made about spelling.

It is not possible to teach every pattern or to help students be aware of every possible spelling generalization. This does not matter. The knowledge that patterns do exist, that spelling is not random and illogical, can give power to young and struggling spellers. When they come to an unfamiliar word, they will not have to make wild guesses or choose a simpler word; they will try to make the links that make spelling possible. If the students come up with the wrong result, they will know that they have alternate strategies to use.

A pattern* can be presented as a list of words that share a common spelling element; it tells you what combinations of letters are possible. A generalization* is something each person must make independently. A generalization is the knowledge that tells you that a word you want to spell is similar to several others you know and likely follows the same pattern. It tells you what is probable. Collecting word families and grouping words can draw students' attention to patterns. Once they have made the appropriate generalization, the students will be able to apply it to new words in the future.

As often as possible, have students make links among words:

- Try not to teach words singly. If you write a word for a student, always try to write two or three others that fit the same pattern. Ask the student to generate more words for the list.
- If a student asks how to spell a word, try to help him or her determine the spelling by suggesting other words that might share spelling elements. Ask questions: do you know any other words which have the same sound? do you know any other similar words? what other words do you know that might be linked in meaning? Even if the student cannot arrive at the correct spelling, you will be teaching a strategy for figuring out words.
- Have students sort and classify words according to spelling pat-

---

* In England, you would find *woollen*: in North America, it is written *woolen*.
* for example, *play, lay, may, clay, tray, say*
* for example, a long "a" sound at the end of words is often spelled "ay"

terns. Ask them to justify the ways they have sorted. This justification is often a spelling generalization, for example, "I put these together because they all have double consonants".

- Use correct spelling terminology, such as "consonant" and "long/short vowel". Terminology is not difficult to learn when used in the context of talking about language. Knowing these words will enable you and the students to talk about parts of words.
- Talk through your own spelling processes as you write on the board, for example, "I always remember the 'c' in *medicine* because it goes with *medical*."

Pronunciation Cues

Sometimes letters appear in words to help in pronunciation. Consider the following rule:

"i" and "e" soften "c" and "g"

This gives us words like:

civil	cent
prestigious	general

This also tells us that any other vowel following "c" or "g" will give a hard consonant:

cat	cucumber	cod
gain	gullible	gopher

This can help when we are adding endings. As an example: if you follow the regular rule for adding "ing" to *picnic*, you would get *picnicing*. This would be pronounced "picnissing", therefore we have to add a "k" — *picnicking, trafficking, mimicking,* and *politicking*.

Another example: if you added an "ous" ending to *courage*, following the usual rule, you would have *couragous*. This would have to be pronounced with a hard "g", so we do not drop the "e":

courageous, outrageous

but   raging and aging are correct

If we remember what "i" and "e" do to pronunciation, we can avoid numerous common spelling errors.

The best way to learn this kind of spelling generalization is by collecting words and putting them into categories, for example:

noticeable   replaceable   serviceable   knowledgeable

Origins and Derivations

Engage your students' interest in spellings by telling them about word origins. This information could start a research project as the students find answers to their questions and collect more word origins.

- Numerous words have come from people's names:

Louis Braille   Rudolf Diesel   Nicholas Chauvin
Samuel Maverick   Friedrich Mesmer   Teddy Roosevelt
Amelia Bloomer   Charles Boycott   Ambrose E. Burnside
Louis Pasteur   Andre Ampere   Saint Audrey*
Robert Bunsen   James Watt

- You will never know how close you came to eating a peanut butter Montague. If you want to know why, find out about the origin of the sandwich.
- Many words have come into English from other languages. Here are a few examples:

from Native American:	raughroughoun (raccoon)	isquontersquashe (squash)
from Innuit	kayak	
from Norse	knife	hut
from Latin	exit	fan (fanaticus)
from Hindu	pyjama	gymkhana
from Greek	atomic	drama
from Malay	gingham	ketchup
from Chinese	tea	mandarin
from Japanese	kimono	typhoon
from Portuguese	banana	molasses
from Arabic	algebra	zero
from Gaelic	slogan	clan
from Spanish	rodeo	mosquito
from Hebrew	camel	cinnamon
from Dutch	wagon	yacht

---

* These last three gave us the following words: teddy bear, sideburns, and tawdry, used to describe lace sold at her fair.

from German	kindergarten	sauerkraut
from Italian	umbrella	piano
from Russian	sputnik	glasnost
from Iranian	shawl	sandal

- French was introduced to England after the Norman conquest in 1066. For several generations after that, French was the language of the ruling class, English that of the servant and peasant class.* Hence, our alternate names for cooked and raw meat: the lord, who saw the meat cooked, used the French word, while the servant/farmer, who saw it raw, used the English word.

cow	beef (boeuf)
sheep	mutton (mouton)
pig	pork (porc)

Words used in everyday life tended to be English, for example, *man, day, drink, sleep, love, water,* while the words of government, leisure, and the law tended to be French: *parliament, justice, pleasure, castle, chivalry.*

- Many words came from the names of places:

| Cologne | Kashmir | Frankfurt | Tabasco |
| Hamburg | Manila | Tangier | Nimes* |

- Lewis Carroll, in *Through the Looking Glass,* started the custom of making portmanteau words, by combining two existing words. Now we have words like these:

glimmer	(glare + shimmer)
medicare	(medical + care)
smash	(smash + bash)
flare	(flame + glare)
twirl	(twist + swirl)

- We have acronyms, words created from initials:

| radar | sonar | scuba | cobol* |

- Computer science has introduced new vocabulary. We now "access information", "interface" with one another, and want things to be "user-friendly".

---

* Latin was the language of the church.
* Serge de Nimes = denim
* **R**adio **D**etection **A**nd **R**anging
Sound **N**avigation and **R**anging
Self **C**ontained **U**nderwater **B**reathing **A**pparatus
Common **B**usiness **O**riented **L**anguage

Not only is this kind of information interesting, it helps us make first meaning, and then spelling links.

Visualizing

A stratagem many people use when trying to figure out how to spell a word is to write it two or more ways and see which looks best. If we have a reasonably good sense of what is possible, this can help to eliminate the incorrect spelling. Do not assume that your students will automatically do this; they may think that looking a word up in a dictionary is the only legitimate way to check spelling. Teach them that this stratagem is often practised by adults. If the students can select the right spelling from the alternatives they have written, they develop more confidence in their own spelling knowledge.

Using the Dictionary

How many times have we heard the plea, "How can I look up a word if I don't know how to spell it?" We use a dictionary for two main purposes: to check the spelling of a word, and to find out what a word means. In both instances, the spelling of a word helps us locate it. It would seem that for poor spellers, a dictionary is less than useful. Not so.

Finding Your Way Around the Dictionary

Finding a word in a dictionary requires two pieces of information:

a knowledge of alphabetical order
the first few letters of the word (at least)

Alphabetical order is easy to teach; there are plenty of rhymes and alphabet picture books. Many of us have learned to say it backwards, a useful trick for dictionary searching. You can almost make a rhyme of it:

Z Y X and W V,
U T S and R Q P
O N M and L K J
I H G

F E D
C B A.

(We did say almost.)

If you watch young children searching for a word in a dictionary, you will notice they often read in the same way they read other books — they start at the beginning and keep going until they find what they are looking for. This method does not work well for reference material. Students need to know that all reading is not the same; they cannot always work in chronological order. The students need a sense of location of letters within the alphabet. Teach them some basic search skills:

- For young children, alphabetize objects in the room: label equipment containers, coathooks, tote boxes, writing folders, mailboxes. Have the students use the alphabet to find things.
- Assign a letter to a student. Ask him or her to open the dictionary to that letter. How close can he or she come? The students can work in pairs and challenge each other.
- Some students may find it useful to use their own names in dictionary searches. If they can open a dictionary near where their own name would appear, they can use that as a baseline, searching either before or after this letter. This skill is useful unless a name is near the beginning or the end of the alphabet. (At least we have two or more names to use.)
- Some larger and more expensive dictionaries have indented tabs to show where letters begin. Try to have at least one of these dictionaries in the room for student usage. The students can get used to locating the initial letter, before trying to find the whole word.
- Teach the students to use the guide words. Give a word, then ask them to find not the word, but the page it is on. This activity can also be practised in pairs.
- Make dictionary usage a normal part of everyday classroom life. The more familiar a dictionary becomes, the easier it will be to use.
- Have available as many different dictionaries as you can. Students should know that not all dictionaries provide the same service: on some occasions a pocket version is sufficient, while on other occasions, they will need a comprehensive dictionary.

Search skills are important. If it takes too long to find a word, the students will not find the dictionary useful.

The first principle is a **most of the time** rule. Consonant sounds tend to be reliable; if a word sounds as if it starts with "t", chances are it starts with "t".

If this rule lets you down when you go to the dictionary, it is necessary to use an alternate stratagem. This involves knowing what the possible alternatives are, and where you should look first:

- If it sounds as if it starts with "f", and it doesn't, it will start with "ph".
- If it sounds as if it starts with "n", and it doesn't, try "kn" (the most likely alternative), then try "gn" (much rarer), then try "pn" (these are all scientific or medical, and all start with "pneu"), and, as a last resort, try "mn" (*mnemonic* is the only one in our dictionary; use *memory* and *amnesia* as cues).
- If it sounds as if it starts with "k", and it doesn't, try "c" (most common). Then try "ch" (rare).
- If it sounds like "kw", try "qu".
- If it sounds as if it starts with "j", and it doesn't, try "g".
- If it sounds as if it starts with "r", and it doesn't, try "wr" before trying "rh".
- If it sound sounds if it starts with "s", and it doesn't, try "ps" (pseudo, psycho, psalm).
- If it sounds as if it starts with "t", and it doesn't, try "p" (most of us will never encounter this, unless we have an interest in exotic beasts).*
- If it sounds as if it starts with "o", and it doesn't, try "h".
- If it sounds as if it starts with a particular vowel, and it doesn't, try all the other vowels until you find it. Vowels are often unpredictable.

Also remember:

- "q" is always followed by "u".
- "w" is often followed by "h".
- Many vowel sounds can be represented by different combinations of vowels. You may have to hunt around.

---

* Like Pteradons and ptarmigans

A few basic alternatives like these will allow you to find your way around a dictionary. The more skilled you become at knowing alternatives, the less time it will take you to find a word. Until you can remember these tips, you might keep a cheat sheet inside your dictionary as reference. It should tell you what the possible alternatives are, and in which order you should try them. It might look like this:

F	PH			
J	G			
K	C		CH	QU
N	KN	GN	PN	MN
R	WR	RH		
S	PS			
T	PT			
O	HO			
Q	+U			
W	+H			

Most unpredictable and silent groups of letters, such as "ght", come later in a word. As students learn more about these patterns of spelling, they will be able to find words more quickly. Until that time, knowing the first part of a word will help get them started.

Proofreading

When we were in school, the teacher was the copy editor, proofreading our writing as part of the marking process. We had no chance to do our own proofreading because for us writing was a one-shot operation; everything was supposed to come out right the first time. Once the teacher had isolated all the errors, we were expected to do the corrections. This was seen as a disgrace and a punishment; little learning was attached to the correction process. The most obvious lesson was that the less we wrote, and the simpler the words we used, the fewer mistakes we were likely to make. This lesson did not make better writers, nor better spellers.

Rather than perpetuating this system, we want to teach our

students that proofreading and editing are the final and necessary steps in the writing process. We teach them the *why* of proofreading by providing many opportunities for them to share and display their writing. We teach them the *when* of proofreading by focusing on editing only when composition and organization are complete. Let us now look at the *how* of proofreading.

We know that even good spellers sometimes read through their work and do not spot all the spelling mistakes. You may have already spotted a proofreading slip in this book; it is difficult and time-consuming to be perfect. Readers are constantly predicting what ideas, information, or words will come next as they look for meaning in the text. A reader does not need to look too closely at much of the visual information on the page; much of it can be taken as understood. This is one reason why fluent readers do not always learn about spelling as they read — they move quickly to meanings, and do not notice the details of letters and words. This is also why good readers and spellers can sometimes make poor proofreaders.

On the other hand, it is not possible to be a good proofreader without looking at the meaning and language the writer is trying to convey. A proofreader often needs to consider the meaning, the part of speech, the tense and so on, to know if a word is spelled correctly. You cannot proofread by reading a text backwards and looking at the words one at a time. Proofreading has its own group of skills which need to be practised.

You can teach your students to become better proofreaders. Here are several stratagems you can suggest:

- Look **for**, rather than **at**. Do not just read over the writing — look for specific things. Your own experience will gradually teach you what kinds of errors to look for.
- Know which words cause trouble for you, and look out for them. Build your own cheat sheet as a reference for these words.
- Recognize homophones and give them some extra thought. As an example, if you have written *there*, make sure that the spelling is correct.
- Offer your help as a proofreader for a classmate. You do not need to be an expert speller to do this. Perhaps all you need to say is, ''Are you sure about this word?''
- Proofread only when all composition and organization is complete. Then you can focus on spelling only.
- Even if you cannot find every error, do the best you can. Ask

for help with the others. You will get more proficient as you go along.

Spelling Trivia

- Some of Noah Webster's "improved" spellings, which were later taken out of his dictionary, included: *bilt, tung, breth, helth, iz, relm, beleeve, mashine, wimmin*, and *yeer*.
- *Poodle* and *puddle* have the same origin. *Poodle* comes from the German word *pudelhund*, meaning "splash dog".
- Would you mark these words as spelling errors?
  astroid crysal galop orchestia tecnology warehous windrow
  They are not misspellings, but are all real words:
  — an adjective meaning "star-shaped"
  — part of an archery bow
  — a 19th-century German dance
  — a genus of crustacean
  — the study of children
  — fishes, the plural of "warehou"
  — a row of hay raked together to dry
- *Daffodil* comes into English from Dutch, which is hardly surprising, as the Netherlands is famous for bulbs. What may be surprising is that our meaning of daffodil is the result of a mistake. *Affodil* is derived from the Greek *Asphodel*, meaning "flower".
- *Caterpillar* comes from two Latin words, *catta* and *pilosus*, meaning "hairy cat".
- Word meanings often change over time:
  — *girl* and *niece* used to refer to either a boy or a girl.
  — *pipe* used to mean any musical instrument.
  — to *starve* meant to die
  — *lumber* used to mean a room for wood
  — *meat* used to mean any food
  — *bible* used to mean any book.
- Sports fans may be interested in these derivations:
  — *racket*, from the Arabic *rahat*, meaning "palm of the hand".
  — *score*, from the Old Norse word, *notch*. Scores were kept by making notches in wood. We retain this meaning when we use *score* when referring to marking lines in wood or paper.
  — *arena*, from the Latin *harena*, meaning "sand".

- We have adopted words from Greek myths, for example, *Atlas, Nemesis, Tantalus,* and *Achilles.*

If you find this kind of word trivia interesting, you have something in common with most people. Background knowledge gives colour and meaning to our language.

Most of us enjoy playing with words, whether through board games, circle games, crossword puzzles, or puns. Much of our humour is founded on the ambiguity and flexibility of words. Words have their own fascination, and the more you know, the more interesting they become. Also, the more you know about words, the better you will be able to make the connections necessary for spelling them correctly.

Spelling need not only be seen as a by-product of writing. The study of words as entities in themselves is a valid and interesting subject for study in the classroom.

How To Remember
Study Skills

If there is a particular word a student wishes to memorize, you might suggest some or all of the following:

- Print the word and keep it in a handy place to refer to whenever you need it. Repeated use will help memorization.
- Several times a day, try to write the word from memory, then check and see if you were right.
- Note which parts of the word you misspell, and concentrate on these. Feel good about the number of letters you do get in the right place.
- Look at the word for 15—30 seconds. Close your eyes gently so you can continue to "see" the word. Then write the word and see if you were right.
- Invent a way to pronounce the word that will help you with spelling, for example, say "Wed nes day", in order to remember all the letters, and "ne k essary" to remember the order of "c" and "ss" in *necessary*.
- Print words you are trying to visualize, rather than writing them in script. Printed letters are more distinctive, and stand out as individuals. Young children often prefer to work with upper case letters as they are distinct from one another. "B" and "D" are easier to distinguish between than are "b" and "d".

• When you find a method that helps you, share it. Talking about the method will help you, and perhaps your listener too.

Mnemonic Devices

A mnemonic device is a trigger that makes a link between words and spellings and can help one remember seemingly illogical and random spellings.

The best mnemonic device is one you think up for yourself, one that has a significant meaning that will come to mind when you need it. It may be as personal as remembering that *phone* starts like "Phenix"; this would not be useful for most people, but can be infallible for a few of us.

Sometimes we adopt another person's mnemonic trigger if we find it memorable. Encourage the students to share their own tricks and secrets. You can also suggest triggers to students, ones that have worked for you. It is not profitable, however, to ask students to memorize the secrets. The whole point of a mnemonic device is that you think of it instantly when it is needed. If the mnemonic device cannot be remembered easily, it will not be useful.

Here are some examples of mnemonics which have worked for some people:

Hear cl**ear**ly with your **ears**.
U and **I** b**ui**ld a house.
I'll be your fri**end** til the **end**.
Age is advant**age**ous.
A **beach** is by the **sea**: a **beech** is a tr**ee**.
A **pie**ce of **pie**.
The princi**pal** is your **pal**.
I like my j**uice** with **ice**.

What Not To Learn

We no longer consider it possible in our schools to make a list of all the facts a person needs to know to be considered educated. We likely never could, but we tried anyway. Today, we are more concerned with teaching problem-solving strategies so students will be able to cope with whatever situations they will meet in their worlds. We teach our students how to find the information they need, rather than relying on rote learning. What is important is *to know what to do with information, how to use it to solve problems as they arise.*

In teaching spelling, we have come to recognize that rote learning of a few selected words does not enable our students to solve future spelling problems. Even if it were possible for all students to memorize the 3 000 most commonly-used words, these would represent only a fraction of the words they will use in their writing. We know, too, that many students cannot memorize all the words on a list, while others can only remember the words for as long as it takes to do the test. It is the application of spelling knowledge to new words that is the useful skill. Knowing how spelling works, how to proofread, and how to use a dictionary, are more important spelling skills than a few memorized words.

We know that rote memorization is the most difficult way to learn anything, the most boring, and the least motivating. Moreover, it often produces learning that is short-lived. Things we have learned by rote are only retained by the memory if they are important to us, if they are used constantly, or if they have engaged our interest for some reason. We remember facts like the alphabet and our telephone numbers because we use the information regularly. We remember other people's phone numbers if we call them frequently enough. Have you noticed, though, that when you move, you quickly forget the phone number you have remembered and used for years? We remember favourite poems and songs from our childhood, but the poems we were assigned to memorize did not stay with us for long.

Students will learn many words by memorizing them. They learned to write their own names in this way, first by copying them and then by repeating them so many times that the spelling became automatic. When the students were at a beginning stage in invented spelling, many knew some sight words because they had seen and written them repeatedly, words like *the* and *my*. Students learned these words because they needed them; they remembered them because they used them and so re-memorized them constantly. Words that are useful for us or have significance in our lives are likely to be remembered.

Many words can be learned only by memorization. Many of

the most commonly-used words fall into this category, words like *why*, *because*, and *eight*. Since these words will be used over and over again, it is worthwhile to spend time learning them. Because we use them repeatedly, there is a good chance that they will pass into long-term memory and become automatic for us. However, if at any time we cease to use them, they may, like our old telephone numbers, fade from our minds.

Because rote learning is so difficult and transitory, we should use it as little as possible. Fortunately in spelling, we have other methods to help us remember words.

Most words fall at least in part into some kind of group. Even *because* has three predictable consonants and an easy-to-spell first syllable. If we think of the meaning and derivation — be the cause — this may also help the spelling. Few words need to be learned in total isolation from other words. Whenever possible, words should be linked together in their natural spelling patterns. Learning about one word can give information about many other words.

4. Teaching Strategies

Individual and Group Teaching

By using different groupings and modes of instruction, you can address three major goals:

Individual	Help with spelling problems a student is encountering at the moment in a particular piece of writing.
Small Group	Have students learn and share strategies for learning about words, and solving spelling problems.
Whole Class	Enlarge the students' knowledge base in order to help them solve spelling problems in the future.

A balanced program makes the most of all three modes of teaching.

Individual

A writing conference provides a prime time for you to teach spelling concepts students need to know at a relevant moment. When all the composing and organizing have been done, you and the student can focus completely on spelling information. This information can then be applied to the writing, perhaps as a proofreading activity. Students are more likely to understand

and remember information when they see a need for it immediately than if they try to learn it in isolation for future reference. Spelling concepts taught in the conference with direct reference to a student's writing have a good chance of being understood and remembered, especially if they are used frequently in future writing.

Here are some ways you can teach spelling as part of a writing conference:

- For a very young student who has not yet begun to attempt writing, you might print as he or she dictates. This models the act of writing, and demonstrates that writing preserves your language and message.
- Help students who are at an early stage of invented spelling to listen for, and print, the consonant sounds of words.
- Demonstrate letter shapes for those who have not yet learned them.
- Provide spellings of a few specific words the student needs for the piece.
- ''Talk through'' the spelling as you make suggestions, for example, ''*Shave* starts with the same sound as your name. What are the two letters you should use?''
  ''This is spelled 'sigh'. You could think of it along with *sight* and *night*. Do you know of any others that might be the same?''
  ''This is the name of a place. It needs a capital letter.''
- Pick out one or two spelling patterns you could teach, for example, ''This word ends in 'dge'. Here is another word which also ends in 'dge'. What other words might end this way? Notice they all have short vowels in the syllable. All words like this have 'dge', not just 'ge'.''
- Suggest words or concepts to proofread, for example, if there are some common words the student constantly misspells, write them down or help the student start a cheat sheet as a reference. Next time, ask the student to proofread for those words.
- If a student is having difficulty with proofreading, mark the beginning of lines that contain errors you think the student should notice, and ask him or her to find and correct the errors.
- Look for patterns in spelling errors, and direct the student's attention to them. It might be adding verb endings, making plurals, or doubling consonants. If students are aware of possible problems, they can proofread for these specific items. If

they are aware of *types* of errors they make, the students can concentrate on learning a group of words or a spelling concept.

- Point out interesting aspects of words a student has used. It might be a Greek or Latin origin, or a word that has come into English from another language. You may be able to draw a parallel with a word in French or Spanish. This kind of information can help students understand how words are related to one another, as well as how languages are related.
- If a student is worried about spelling, take opportunities to point out correct spellings and areas of progress. Set realistic proofreading and correcting goals for the student so the task does not become overbearing.

Small Group Instruction

Group instruction might be specially arranged for the purpose of spelling, but there are many opportunities to teach about spelling whenever a group of students is gathered together. This might be for a reading or writing activity, a research project, a science experiment, or any time words are being used.

- When a student is sharing a piece of writing during a group conference, suggestions you make about spelling will be attended to by the other students.
- If one student needs help with spelling during a group conference, the other students might be involved in the learning. As an example, ask, "What other words do you know that might start with 'ch'?"
- Have the students bring along for discussion specific pieces of their own writing you or they have selected on the basis of spelling problems.
- Have the students work in groups to solve spelling problems.
- Have the students work in small groups to research spellings, word origins, and so on. They can then pass on what they have learned to another group or to the whole class.
- Encourage the students to work in pairs at the editing stage of their writing. They can help each other proofread and use reference sources.
- Have the students share their strategies for spelling. They could talk about which words cause them problems, how they remember difficult words, how they figure out new words. The

more ways students hear of solving spelling problems, the better they will be able to solve their own.

- Bring together small groups of students who share the same spelling problem, for example: you may notice several students who can not spell contractions. Have them bring to the meeting a piece of their own writing that uses contractions. You can then teach a lesson using the students' own examples, and have the students help one another to edit their writing. You could bring the same group together two weeks later to see whether they are applying their new learning, and whether they need more help.

Whole Class Instruction

Large group sessions provide opportunities for you to teach concepts and information about spelling which you might not be able to do during a writing conference. As an example, Greek or Latin influences on our spelling and language are interesting and useful, especially as prefixes and suffixes, but you may not want to wait until they appear in a student's writing. In a large group session, you can give information and teach concepts of more general use to raise students' awareness of words and language. Whenever you increase students' knowledge and awareness of language, you are helping them understand how to construct words. The more the students know, the more intelligent will be their predictions when they spell unfamiliar words.

Large group instruction should be confined to those concepts everyone needs or can be involved with. This might include such things as information about origins, meanings, patterns, derivations, and word construction. Everyone can be involved — good spellers will be able to contribute words and ideas — others can be helped to understand new concepts and make new generalizations. Instruction should generally be short and focus on one topic only.

Do not confine the teaching of spelling to a particular time or place. When you use a word ending in ''ology'' in your science class, talk about the origin and meaning of this suffix and start your students on a word collection. Most of the time you will have a different focus for your teaching, and will not want to divert attention to spelling. Sometimes, however, you may want to take a few minutes, choose one spelling concept, and teach a mini-lesson.

Here are some ways you can involve your whole class in spelling learning:

- For beginning spellers, draw their attention to initial consonants in a chart story or Big Book. Ask them to suggest other words that start with the same sound.
- Choose a word from a reading experience, and use it as a model to teach a spelling concept or pattern, for example: "*Jumped* sounds as if it ends in 't', but it doesn't. It is always 'ed'. Let's make a list of words we know with this ending."
- Teach a word or concept all the students need for a specific task, for example: if all the students are going to write and mail a letter, print the school address on the board, along with the words, *Dear* and *yours sincerely*. After the letters are written, draw the students' attention to the "ly" ending and how it is added to words. The students could suggest other examples for you to list or work in small groups to make their own lists.
- Pick out a particular prefix or suffix encountered in reading, writing, or discussion. Teach the meaning and derivation, and ask the students to suggest other words in which it is used. You or the students can list the words and display them.
- Talk about what you are doing when the students are watching you write on the board: "These are called 'periods'. They show when I am ending one sentence, and starting another. Where do you think the next one should go?"
- Talk about how you work out spellings when you write on the board, for example: "This 'kw' sound is always spelled 'qu'. *Quiet* starts like *queen* and *quick*." "I remember to put 'ery' on *stationery* because I think of the 'er' in *paper*."

These three modes of teaching are all appropriate in a classroom spelling program. They may be incidental as opportunities and needs arise or they might be planned for in special times set aside. A well-planned program strikes a balance between general spelling instruction designed to broaden the students' knowledge, and specific instruction designed to help a student with a piece of writing.

The Spelling Period

The Spelling Period has fallen into disrepute because it is associated with the rote learning of word lists and the Friday test. This kind of spelling instruction does more harm than good. Not only does it teach little of worth; it often takes valuable time away from reading and writing, activities far more likely to teach about spelling.

This does not mean, however, that having a special time for teaching spelling is wrong. There is much to be gained by sometimes making spelling the prime focus for the students, rather than always being incidental to some other task. It is the *content* of the lessons that have been wrong, not the *concept*. Here are some guidelines for making the spelling period a meaningful learning situation for your students:

- First, engage the students in the fascination of words and language. To learn, the students must want or need to know.
- Keep the instruction time short, perhaps five to ten minutes.
- Have your spelling period only once or twice a week.
- Choose only one spelling concept as the focus of your lesson, for example, a topical word, a suffix, a rhyming pattern, or a dictionary skill. Do not feel obliged to have a list of words to study. You may deal with only one word, you may have a short list of sight words (for example, months, scientific terminology), you may build a category with dozens of words. It is the concept you are teaching.
- Always link words in a spelling context. Use words that share a spelling pattern, a meaning link, or derivation.
- Choose words and concepts the students are likely to need in their writing.
- Focus on investigation and problem solving, not memorization.
- Do not make a test the goal of spelling learning.
- Have students apply their new learning as quickly as possible. This might be in proofreading their own writing for a specific spelling pattern, collecting or categorizing words, solving puzzles, discussing the new concept in groups, using reference materials, reading, or researching.
- Encourage the students to relate the spelling concept to their own writing.

The Spelling Journal

A spelling journal can enable a student to build a personal spelling text and dictionary that can then serve as a reference book and a teaching aid. This is particularly useful for older students and for adults. The journal could include the following:

- A personal dictionary of hard-to-spell words. A page could be allocated to each letter of the alphabet. The student could list words with a particular difficulty or that he or she has looked up in a dictionary. This will build a cheat sheet, a quick reference for the future. When various words are no longer problematic, they could be checked off. An increasing number of deleted words will give confidence that learning is taking place.
- If a student comes up with a mnemonic device or a hint for remembering a spelling pattern, this could be recorded in the journal.
- Thoughts, feelings, and frustrations could be recorded. An understanding of why spelling causes anxiety can help a student take a more rational approach to understanding the place of spelling. This can help him or her to separate spelling from the composing process, and allow writing to continue unhindered by spelling problems.
- Rules and patterns a student is trying to learn could be recorded in a special place in the journal. Possible examples include: "ity" or "ety"? — add "ity" unless the preceding letter is an "i". (exceptions are *nicety* and *subtlety*)
  "cede", "sede", or "ceed"? — add "cede".
  (exceptions are *supersede, exceed, proceed, succeed*)
- Demon words, those that are common and troublesome, can be listed. They can be used as a reference, and as a list for study.
- Facts about words and spellings the student finds interesting can be recorded. These could be words origins, unusual spellings, information about spelling reform, reviews of "How To Be a Better Speller" books, or the names of famous writers who admit to being poor spellers (F. Scott Fitzgerald, John Irving).
- The students can record topics discussed in conferences with peers or the teacher, and suggestions for future action or study.
- Students can record their own successes, and build up a catalogue of things they are learning about spelling.

The Personal Dictionary

The dictionary is such a basic tool of spelling that all older students should have one of their own. It can be a workbook, as well as a reference book. It should be large enough to have a good range of words, and have enough white space in which to make notes and notations. The spelling journal may be used in conjunction with this dictionary to make longer notes. The dictionary may be used to do the following:

- Make a mark beside a word that you look up for spelling. It might be a dot or the date. If you come to look the same word up again, make another mark. You will soon get to know which words give you trouble. Words you need to look up regularly are words worth learning.
- A dictionary usually provides derivations and origins of words. This information can be useful in learning the spelling, as well as the meaning. Looking up one word can help you to spell a group of related words.
- Dictionaries also give information on pronunciation. Pronouncing all parts of a word correctly can help in spelling. It is worthwhile to learn how to read the pronunciation cues. Practise articulating words correctly.
- If you look up a word with a prefix, you will usually find a long list of other words which use the same prefix. Knowing the meaning and the spelling can help spell these other words. This kind of "many for the price of one" learning can give spelling confidence. Notes on other useful words with the same prefix can be recorded in the spelling journal.
- When you look up a word in a dictionary, you usually read several other words on the same page. This can spark an interest in new and unusual words and broaden your vocabulary. You might find a word you can try to use during the course of the day.

One word of caution about dictionaries. If they are used extensively during first draft writing, they can hinder the flow of composition. A student who goes to the dictionary frequently in the early stages of writing is a student who is afraid of making a spelling mistake, and who does not understand the drafting and process aspects of writing. Young children often give themselves away when they are constantly asking, ''How do you spell

_____ ?'' or search for words listed around the room before they attempt to write them.

If you see this kind of over-dependence on correct spelling on first-draft writing, encourage the student to make his or her best attempt at the word, perhaps making a note to check the spelling at a convenient time. In extreme cases, ban dictionaries until the first draft is complete. If you do this, you must never comment on spelling, except to offer help, until the student has had a chance to check and correct. Once he or she understands when correct spelling is appropriate, then you can relax the rules.

Collections

Once students are aware that two or three words may work in the same way, they can begin collections. Collecting words helps students form generalizations about how words are spelled. Learning words in groups can help students link words together to remember spellings. Knowing that by learning one word you can now spell many other words gives a sense of power and control over the many alternatives in spelling.

Here some examples to show how you can use collections to raise spelling awareness:

- Suppose the students have been reading or reciting, ''Humpty Dumpty''. Ask them, ''which word rhymes with *wall*?'' Print *fall* on the board. Then ask them to suggest any other words they know which rhyme with *wall*. You could leave the list up for a few days, so that students can add more rhyming words as they find them in their reading. Students who know the initial consonants you have used will be able to read the words on the list. Very soon, even young students will be able to work in pairs or small groups to make their own lists of words which follow a pattern. Sometimes, the students will suggest a word that sounds as if it fits the pattern, but is spelled differently. As an example, someone might suggest *doll*. You must then tell them that this word doesn't fit the pattern. Write it off to one side by itself. In some cases, this can be the start of a whole new pattern.
- Ask the students to call out all the words they can think of that have the /ee/ sound, as in *feet*. Print the words on chart paper (some will have ''ee'', some will have ''ea'', some will have

"ei"). When you have listed all the words the students can think of, ask them what is different about the words. Have two or three students cut out the words on the list and categorize them. The students can then print new lists, showing the different patterns of the /ee/ sound. Each list could then be saved and used as a reference.

- When students work in small groups to generate lists of words that follow a pattern, they will often include words that are an exception to the pattern. The students themselves may be encouraged to discover these words. Someone in the group may question the word's inclusion, and will have to check the spelling. Any time students disagree or are not sure, they should check the spelling. Sharing their lists with other groups or displaying them on the wall will also provide an opportunity for a classmate to question a spelling. In this way, students can learn not to take spellings for granted.
- Students will learn that if a word sounds as if it starts with "n", and it doesn't, there are several possibilities. If they are going to look the word up in the dictionary, the students don't want to waste time. Will they first try "kn", "gn", or "pn"? First, ask them to predict which one they think is the most likely. Then ask them to make a list of all the words they can think of for each. They, and you, may be surprised.*
- Students can work alone or in pairs to find derivational patterns. These might be words sharing the same prefix or the same meaning base, for example: the "uni" words (*uniform, unicycle, unicorn*) or the "two" words (*two, twins, twenty, twice*).

Classification

Classification is an activity that draws attention to patterns and generalizations. Whenever students learn a new word or spelling pattern, it is a good idea to link it with other words which share the same pattern. Here are some examples of activities that ask students to classify words.

---

* For more about dictionary alternatives, see p. 52

- Have a group of students generate a list of words which begin with the hard "c" sound. They should then list them according to the beginning letter, "c" or "k". They could first predict which list they think will be longer. For each word they think of, the students could predict the spelling, check it, and put the word in the appropriate column. The final list will give them useful information about spelling.*
- Give students a number of words and ask them to classify them in as many ways as possible, for example, number of letters, beginning sounds, number of syllables, and meanings. Ask the students to explain and justify their groups. Alternatively, one student can form categories, before asking another to study and explain them. This kind of categorization forces students to examine words and to look for patterns and similarities. (The best way to categorize or classify words is to cut them out and physically move them around. This not only helps the visual learner, it saves a lot of time.) After a classification activity, students could be asked to summarize what they have discovered about spelling.

Exploration

Most people find a certain fascination in words. True investigation comes when the students reflect on why some words are harder to spell than others, how our language developed, and why some games and puzzles present more problems than others. Is it the number of letters? The number of vowels? Do some letters make it harder than other letters? Students should always hold a debriefing after a word game. You will find a lot of spontaneous discussion and arguing during the games as students ask questions and justify decisions.

It is this kind of word investigation that leads to spelling awareness. The way in which students go about finding solutions can be more valuable learning than the answers they find. While they may forget individual words, the students are more likely to remember strategies for discovery. This is the kind of knowledge they can use in the future to solve spelling problems.

---

* Most of the time, use "c". Use "k" only when followed by "i" or "e". (Remember that "i" and "e" soften "c" and "g".) Don't worry about *kleptomaniac*.

Here are some word games and puzzles that encourage students to investigate spellings.

Spelling Trivia

Start to build a Spelling Trivia game with spelling questions like these:

• Which vowel is used most often?
• Which doubled vowel is used most often?
• Which initial consonant is used least often?

Students might like to make up their own trivia questions that can be solved by research. Each question could be put on a file card. The students should share not only their answers, but how they arrived at them.

Word Hunt

This game involves a problem that must be solved by finding words, for example:

• Write words with two "a's", three "a's", four "a's" (try this with any letter).
• Write words with four "a's", four "e's", four "i's", and so on.
• Find words that have all the vowels in them. Try words that have all the vowels in alphabetical order.*
• Write words that have no vowels in them (use "y"). What is the longest word you can find with no vowels?
• Write as many words as you can that contain double vowels: "aa", "ee", "ii", "oo", "uu" (students will discover which are most common/rare).
• For each consonant, try to write a word that has the consonant doubled (some will never double, others will double only in compound words, for example, *fishheads*).
• How many ways can you find to pronounce the name, *Mr. Hough*? Write a rhyming word to demonstrate each pronunciation.*
• Which word ending is the most common: "eat" or "ate"?

---

* Facetiously and abstemiously have all six vowels in alphabetical order.
* For example, Mr. Hoff as in cough.

Word Frame

Give the students a word frame such as those provided below:

r __ __ d   m __ __ t   d __ __ r

Ask the students to fill in the frame to make as many words as possible. They may use dictionaries to find and check words they think of. This investigation will draw their attention to vowels used in combination, and those that are not used in combination.

Word Middles

This is a variation on the word frame. Give the students a group of letters which could be found inside a word, for example, "eat". They must then write as many words as they can with these letters inside, for example, *meat, creation, feature, defeat*.

Consonant-Vowel Clues

In this game, students write clues where only consonants and the number of vowels are given.

- a vegetable that grows underground: "n", "n", and three vowels
- a continent: "r", "p", and four vowels
- an open space: "r", and three vowels
- a province: "n", "t", "r", and four vowels*

When each student in the group has written a few clues, they can be passed to the next person to be solved. Alternatively, you could collect them and make a master list to be duplicated. This might also make a puzzle book for the classroom or school library.

New Words for Old

Ask the students to list all the words they can make from one larger word. To do this, they will need to try different beginnings, middles, and endings. The students will be looking for letter combinations that are likely to occur in words. This is an individual activity, but you can start a master list on which the students

---

* onion, Europe, area, Ontario

can write their words. If you leave the list on the wall, the students will keep adding words as they figure them out.

Crosswords

Crossword puzzles are one of the best ways to explore spelling. As letters of a word fill in, leaving blank spaces between, the possibilities for the missing letters decrease. This can help the students to think of possible and impossible letter groupings. As an example, you have the following:

— — — — — — —

you have no information, most initial letters are possible, but you fill in the "t".

— t — — — — — —

Only a limited number of letters can start the word, and only a limited number can follow the "t".

The word must start with "s" or a vowel (keep "p" in mind just in case).

If you have these letters filled in:

— t — p — a — e

you can figure out that:

- only a consonant can come between the "a" and "e".
- only a consonant can start the word, as a vowel would require a double "t", and this could not be followed by "p".
- the word must start with "s".

s t — p — a — e

- only a vowel can follow the "t".
- there is a very good chance that the letter following the "p" is another "p".*

This is the type of reasoning that goes through one's mind while solving a crossword puzzle. You can help students to figure out the logic of words by working through and discussing a few crosswords on the board. Another option is to have the students work in twos and threes. Group work builds in talk and negotiation, and the students can learn from one another.

---

* The word is *stoppage*.

Games

Parents who have taken children on long car trips know all about the fascination of word games. Here are a few you can revive for the classroom:

I Packed My Bag

This is a circle game, best played in a small group of two to five people. The first person starts by saying, ''I packed my bag, and in it I put an apple'' (something starting with 'a'). The second person continues by repeating the first item, and adding one starting with ''b'', ''I packed my bag, and in it I put an apple and a beaver.'' The game works best when the players help each other out when the string of words starts to get long. You can make this a co-operative game by having everyone in the group repeat the list each time, allowing the next player in turn to add a word. In this way, everyone participates all the time. This version can be played with larger groups because no one has to wait for a turn.

Word String

This is also a circle game for a small group. The first person says a word, the second person follows with a word starting with the last letter of the previous word. No repetitions are allowed. The idea is to make a long string of words. They can be written down. Players soon get to know which letters are more difficult to start words with, and start planning ahead to catch the next person out.

You can make the game more advanced by introducing a theme, for example, the words must all be animals, countries, or a type of food. You can add another element by providing reference books, asking for the string of words to be written down, and allowing two or three sessions for the string to be completed. This is a good co-operative game for groups to see how long they can make a theme list. The students may find, for example, that they can make their list potentially longer by rearranging their words.

Beetle

This used to be called "Hangman", but as the concept isn't pleasant, we've renamed it. This is a game for two players. One thinks of a word and writes down a dash for each letter in the word. The other player then has to figure out the word by suggesting one letter at a time. Only one guess at the complete word is allowed. If the suggested letter is not in the word, a part of the beetle is drawn. The finished beetle looks like this:

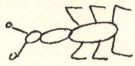

It will have three body parts, six legs, and two antennae. This allows for eleven guesses to fill in letters.

Students quickly learn which are the most commonly-used vowels and consonants, and which go together in combinations. This is a particularly good game for older students. They learn that once you have any letters in a word, options for other letters are dramatically reduced. The more letters there are, the easier the prediction becomes, until there is only one possible answer. The game is excellent for teaching possible and probable letter sequences.

Concentration

This is an individual game. One person chooses a word, and discovers how many other words can be made from the letters, for example, we came up with sixty-two words from *Saskatchewan*. A variation is to print the word on chart paper and put it on the wall for a few days. The students can then add words as they discover them.

When you are teaching these games to the students, you might consider teaching a small group of five, then sending each of the five off to teach the game to a group. You will probably find the groups coming up with "local rules" to solve problems as they arise.

Ask your students to bring to school any word games their families know, and teach the class how to play. In this way, you can build up a collection.

Another interesting and challenging project is for the students to make their own word-game book for the classroom in which they write the instructions for the games. Writing instructions is a demanding task. Audience reaction will soon tell the writers if they have omitted an important point, if they have not provided clear explanations, or have put information in the wrong order. As a final edit, each game should be played according to the written instructions. The students can make any necessary changes to their descriptions and print their final draft.

Commercial Games

Games like Scrabble™ and Lexicon™ are useful additions to your spelling sessions. Any game that requires participants to manipulate letters and words is likely to build word awareness and spelling knowledge.

Computer-Assisted Spelling

Many people think that using a computer to check and correct spellings is somehow cheating; that spelling must be done manually. This view holds only for students, of course; no one would suggest that a publishing company or a professional writer not use electronic proofreading. Like the pocket calculator and the secretary, labour-saving gadgets are fine for adults, but students must work the hard way.

This is a very limited view, both of what can be learned by using a computer, and of the place of spelling in the writing process.

Both the pocket calculator and a spell-checker program can free students from the tyranny of detail, and allow them to focus on the task of creating meaning. The students can learn problem-solving in math long before they have the computation skills to come up with right answers in a reasonable time. Problem-solving is the major and ultimate goal of a math program, therefore it makes sense to let the students get on with learning to make meaning in math: their skills in computation will catch up eventually. A calculator will not tell you which operations you need to do and in which order, it will not solve problems, but it will perform low-level tasks. For some students, it is not the basic operations of addition, subtraction, multiplication, and division that cause difficulties: it is knowing which operations to perform. Without meaning first, math cannot be done.

Similarly, all young students are able to tell stories, to relate personal experiences, to create imaginary situations, to criticize, to complain, and to express opinions. These are the stuff of composition. When these students start to learn how to write, their ability to spell will lag behind what they have to say for some time. Perhaps most of us compose beyond our ability to formulate language and to spell; this may be one reason so few of us write at all. If we can help students perform the tasks of writing that they have not yet had time to learn, tasks like handwriting and spelling, then we can free them to learn and practise the problem-solving of writing-generating ideas, formulating language, and organizing information. Without the development of these abilities, there is no reason for learning to spell.

A simple word-processing program can help beginning spellers to write. For these students, finding a letter on a keyboard can be faster than printing it with a pencil. Also, recognizing a ''B'' is much easier than remembering how to make one. Young students who have little control over wandering fingers can produce writing that looks perfect to them. This can be highly motivating for a beginner. With only a little learning about letter sounds, the students can produce text that both they and their teacher can read. As the students write, read, and learn more about the patterns of spelling, their ability to spell and print will grow.

Many older students come to see themselves as poor spellers, subsequently drawing the conclusion that they are poor writers. Producing a final draft can be such drudgery that they never want to finish anything. Many students are not risk-takers: even if they are not poor spellers, they are so afraid of making spelling errors that they write as little as possible to diminish their chances of making a mistake. Others are not willing to take spelling risks, and will always write *big* and never try *enormous*. Writing less will not help them learn to spell, and it certainly will not make them better writers.

For these students, using an electronic spell-checker can free them from worrying about spelling mistakes. They can focus on their compositions, use their most adventurous language, and know that spelling errors can be corrected without undue hardship.

Also, the students can learn about the place and relative importance of spelling in the writing process. We must again apply the real-world rules of spelling: for a published book, a billboard, or a business letter, what matters is not *who* fixed up the spelling or *how* it was done. What matters is that it *was* done.

Computer spell-checkers do not do all the work for you. They will not correct your spelling, nor can they tell when you have used a wrong homonym. What most will do is proofread for, and draw your attention to, impossible spellings, before offering alternative spellings. Many have a phonetic input function, before offering suggested alternative spellings. Ultimately, the writer must decide on the basis of his or her own spelling knowledge.

A side-effect of computer spell-checkers is their ability to engage students in word manipulation and discovery. They also make it easy to find words that have similar endings or middles, something an ordinary dictionary cannot do for you. Any time a student asks questions about words, tries alternative ways of working with words and letters, and plays with language, knowledge about spelling is likely to increase. Let us encourage them to make spelling the ultimate video-game.

An acceptance of the principle that we will give students all the help they need to come up with correct spelling easily does not mean that we do not expect them to learn how to do it for themselves. It is a recognition that there is a lot to learn to become a proficient speller, and it is a long process. In the interim, the worst thing that can happen is that a student stops writing. When this happens, learning about spelling, not to mention writing, is no longer possible. Just as we lived happily through the babbling when the young child was learning to talk, so we must live patiently through the years of invented and inaccurate spelling while we give the student time to build up a knowledge of standard forms.

Cheat Sheets

''Cheat Sheet'' is one of the many terms we have adopted from the world of computers. A cheat sheet is a list of facts and information one expects to use often. Our computer manual provides one — a one-page list of the most-needed commands. The purpose of a cheat sheet is to save time checking larger reference sources for facts and information you have not memorized or learned yet.

What usually happens is that once you have looked something up a few times, you remember it, and no longer need the cheat sheet. This makes it a doubly-useful tool for teaching spelling:

- Students can make a list of words they wish to refer to. It might be words they know they have trouble spelling or words they will need for a particular theme or topic. They can easily refer to the list when they are writing, or better still, when they are proofreading. It is quicker and less distracting than using a dictionary.
- After looking up a word several times on the cheat sheet and correcting it in the writing, a student may remember it without looking. Students can also be encouraged to try the word first, then check to see if they are right. When they know the word, it can be taken off the cheat sheet.

The students can make their own cheat sheets for special topics or for their own problem words. You can suggest words during a writing conference as you see a need. You can also provide cheat sheets for commonly-used words, such as days and months, theme words, and service words such as *who, the, what, because*. These could be posted on the wall, printed on file cards, and placed in the writing centre, or made available to individual students who need them.

Sequences of Instruction

We have always looked for ways to make learning easier for our students. One way we have tried to do this is to break learning down into tasks of manageable size and put them into a logical sequence. At first glance, this seems a sensible thing to do.

There are a few snags with this, though. None of us learned language in small chunks presented in a sequence devised by someone else. We learned by being immersed in the whole world of language, none of which made any sense initially. We were the ones who decided what we would learn, in what order we would do it, and whether we would do it or not. We didn't necessarily choose the small words to learn first; we chose the words and phrases we needed at the time, and this was different for each of us. When students are inventing the spellings they need, they will try to spell anything, regardless of the length or difficulty of the word. It is not easy to decide for someone else what is interesting, what is needed, and what is learnable.

Nevertheless, when we are planning a series of lessons for our students, we have to make some arbitrary decisions about what to do and when to do it. It makes sense to try to teach first what the students need to know for the kinds of language tasks they are engaged in. This is why we take the lead from their writing. It also makes sense to do our best to match our teaching with concepts the students are capable of learning.

There are a number of sequences that are worth consideration when planning instruction:

frequently-used words _____	less-common words
single vowel _____	vowel groups
(hat, rest)	(leaf, reign)
single consonant _____	blends and digraphs
sound patterns __ function patterns __ meaning patterns	
recognition of patterns _____	recognition of origins
rhyming relationships _____	derivational relationships
(line, mine, fine)	(muscle, muscular)
playing with words _____	making plays on words
(word games)	(puns, and so on)

In each case, the sequence allows students to build on their existing knowledge and to extend the range of their thinking about words.

It is always important to remember, however, that this progression from easier to more difficult is only a very general overall pattern. Even young students may express complex ideas in sophisticated vocabulary and language if the subject is one they know a lot about or are keenly interested in. We must not hold back concepts and words students need because we feel they are too difficult, or because we think something else ought to be learned first. Only the learner can really decide whether anything is learnable or not. The sensitive teacher will be able to recognize when to continue and when to step back and wait for a more productive learning opportunity

5. Evaluation and Record-Keeping

Evaluating Spelling in Student Writing

When we evaluate spelling, we have two main objectives:

1. Find out what the student knows.
2. Decide what can reasonably be taught.

If we can fulfil these objectives, we can build up a cumulative record of spelling concepts students know, and help them to increase their spelling knowledge.

No arbitrary test will give us useful information about what a student knows, nor about what to teach the student next. The most reliable indicator of spelling proficiency is the student's own writing.

We can look for spelling information in student writing in two ways. The way a student spells during first draft writing will give us some indication of what is automatic for the student and requires little thought. However, when a writer is focusing totally on ideas and language, spelling mistakes are often made inadvertently. When a student has had an opportunity to proofread and correct spelling, we can get a better picture of what the student knows about spelling. We can then decide what we could reasonably expect the student to learn next.

We need to guard against the tendency to try to teach everything a student does not know, to correct every error we see in the spelling. It is our natural urge as teachers to strive for perfection. Perfection, or as near as we can come to it, is obviously a worthwhile goal. However, accurate spelling requires a lot of knowledge and experience. Accumulating and assimilating this knowledge will take many years of example, practice, and instruction. Our students will do a lot of writing before they have learned enough about spelling to even approach accuracy. The last thing we want is for students to limit their writing to words they know they can spell.

As well as deciding what needs to be learned, we must also decide which concepts the student is capable of learning, and how much input he or she can handle at one time. If we expect too much, we run the risk that the student will be overwhelmed, and that there will be no learning. It is better to choose one or two concepts and help the student learn them thoroughly, than to face a student with a catalogue of errors to correct or a long list of words to memorize. If students write regularly, there will be numerous opportunities to teach other concepts later.

Little and often is a good rule for spelling instruction.

Here are some examples that illustrate how you might meet your objectives by analysis of student writing:

Example #1

Morna

MORNA

What the student knows:

— a picture can preserve and convey meaning.
— how to print her name in upper case letters.
— writing is a way of preserving and communicating meaning.
— meaning is represented by squiggles on the page.
— in order to write, you put these squiggles in rows.

What can reasonably be taught:

— ask the student to "read" the story.
— reinforce the fact that the use of correct letters in the name

enables others to read it. Mention the fact that authors always put their names on their work.

— ask about the story told in the picture, so she will generate language to explain, describe, and so on.
— below the picture, print a sentence the author has dictated. Read the ''story'' back. This will show her that language can be preserved by print.
— determine if she knows any other letters, and help her to write them.
— suggest that she visit the library to find some alphabet books.
— do not pressure her to have the story written; sometimes appreciate art for art's sake.
— provide many more opportunities for her to compose meaning through picture.

Example #2

A BOT MI
CH NCHA

MICHNCHA
AZFRE

About my chinchilla. My chinchilla is furry.   Morna

What the student knows:

— every syllable of a word must be represented by letters.
— some sounds are represented by two letters, ''ch''.
— consonant sounds ''b'', ''t'', ''m'', ''n'', ''z'', ''f'', ''r''.
— vowel sounds ''o'', ''a'', ''i'', ''e''.
— this piece has a title, a story, and an illustration. They are separate parts of the writing.

What can reasonably be taught:

— read back the title and story, pointing to each syllable as you go. Reinforce her concept that every syllable is represented.
— begin using the word, *word*. Ask her to tell you where the word *my* ends, and the word, *chinchilla* begins. Show that in books, words are written with spaces in between to make them easier to read. Ask her how many words she has written in her story. Suggest that next time she might try to put spaces between her words. If, on the next occassion, she puts large dots between words, praise this. It will be a short phase.

Example #3

I whis I cieD Be SUPERMan

But i Cant avry time I
asc GoD to ttn me in to SUPERMan
It Duzint Wirk.

Grade One
Seven Years old.

I whis I cied be Superman

What the student knows:

— how to write a complete narrative.
— to represent all the sounds of every word.
— 16 of 23 words are spelled correctly (70 %).
— high frequency words: *i, be, but, me, in, to, it*.
— attempted contraction: "cant".
— long vowel, silent "e": *time*.
— compound word: *Superman*.

What can reasonably be taught:

— "asc", "c" and "k" make the same sound. At the end of words it is almost always "k". Several other words share this pattern: *mask, task, flask . . .*

— "whis", "sh" sound. Many other words share this pattern.
— vowel sound patterns.

Until he has learned more about vowels, learning the sight word *could*, along with *would* and *should* is probably too much for this student. Contractions and punctuation should also be left until later.

Example #4

I was desprat to join the most coolest club in scool, I just had to they said I could but I had to stay over night at the old deserted mantion that everybody said was haunted. I will I told them. As I enterd the mantion I herd a shreek from upstairs. It was pobably just an owl I said to myself, or was it. The mantion was old and dusty. The floors creeked and the wind howled. I went up the stairs very slowly afraid that the stairs would cave in. When I got to the top of the stairs. I saw somthing in the room in front of me. I ran in to the room out of coureosoty, there was nothing there and it was cold in that room how strange. Oh well I better get some rest. Later I heard a scream it woke me up. I finally built up enough courage to look out the window. Althou I could see clearly in the moonlight none was there. Sudenly the fog moved in, and the trees swad even thought there was no wind.

What the student knows:

— how to create mood and build suspense in a narrative. This is the first page of a lengthy story.
— use of periods.
— of 187 words on the page, 171 are spelled correctly (91%).
— how to spell a large number of irregular words: *they, said, could, night, haunted, afraid, heard, some, built, enough, courage, though, there.*
— how to spell a number of compound words: *everybody, overnight, moonlight.*
— how to add endings to root words: *coolest, deserted, haunted, howled, slowly, moved.*

What can reasonably be taught:

— the use of commas as an aid to the reader.
— sight word *school*. Other words share the "sch" spelling pattern, but they are not words she is likely to need.
— "entrd", the pattern for adding "d" or "ed" for past tenses. She might be able to self-correct here, as she is usually good with adding endings.
— *though* is spelled correctly, but "althou" is not. She could be helped to see a link between these two words.
— "shreek/creeked", she has chosen the most common way of spelling the "ee" sound. She might collect words which belong to the same patterns as *shriek* and *creak*.
— words like *desperate, mansion* and *curiosity* could be given if the writing is to be edited in a further draft. Each belongs to a word pattern, but they are not words that are likely to be useful at this stage.

Example #5

The Boy Hwo Found a 20 Doller Bill
   One day I was rideing my bike down the sreet and I saw a loterey ticket. It said if you win you get 1 million dollers. I rode my bike home and gave the lotery ticket to my mom and ran to tell my frends. Wile I was gone to my frends house, the lottery men lochated my house and came over to my house. We won the lottery and now I am in the richest house of them all.

What the student knows:

— how to write a very simple narrative. It has logic and sequence, but no anecdote, description, and so on.
— of 87 words, 76 are spelled correctly (discounting repeated errors)- 87%.
— several irregular words: *one, saw, was, said, won.*
— vowel combination "ou"—*found, house.*
— other vowel combinations—*boy, now, saw, you.*

What could reasonably be taught:

— "wh", give him the group of question words — *who, what, where, when, why.* Add *"while"*. He could keep these as a cheat sheet until he has memorized them.
— "rideing", drop the "e" before adding endings. This generalization can apply to many words.
— ask him to look at the word "sreet" to see if he can self-correct.
— sight words — *dollar, lottery, million, friends, located* — may be given for editing purposes if a final draft is to be written. With such a terse story this is unlikely unless revision is done to flesh out the narrative.

Example # 6

Hello.

Well, I am **writting** to you in order to **determain** the **quallity** of my spelling.

I do have my days **were** I can spell anything, and then there are days that I can't spell a thing. Right now it's a **meadoaker** day.

I am a truck driver so my **writting** and spelling are not practised as much as I'd like. In fact there are times that I lack the confidence to go forth and **conquere** the B.A. of life. It's funny, I graduated from Grade 13, <u>done</u> a year and a half of a management systems program at Lakehead University, and I still cannot spell or express (<u>myself</u>) in proper English. <u>or so</u> called the norm.

My **personel** outlook these days is possibly to go back to school. However I'd like very much to beat this English thing first. I am also at a stage in life where I am not sure of what I'd like to do with the rest of my life. So currently I am exploring avenues, such as teaching Grades 4-6, or maybe finishing my B.A. in **Bussiness** and attempting to get on with a company as a person who isn't a figure head but is a big part of making the company run. I like to be the center of the **cayous**.

I wonder if your job of defining my spelling problem is greatly <u>influence</u> by my poor hand **writting**.

Well, I have definitely talked <u>alot</u> about myself. I'd like to thank you for the time you are putting forth to help me with my problem. So thanks.

Dan

Letter analysis: nine spelling errors (highlighted); five grammar errors (underlined)

This letter was written by an articulate and educated young adult who feels he has a serious problem in spelling. In fact, 96% of the words he has written are spelled correctly, but for the reader the errors in spelling and grammar seem to dominate the text. How may Dan be helped?

First, Dan needs to feel more confident as a speller by recognizing how much he does know:
— he spelled correctly many words which often cause problems: *practised, confidence, graduated, management, possibly, currently, avenues, wonder.*
— he is able to use alphabetic principles to create readable spellings for words he does not know.
— he does not avoid words like *mediocre* and *chaos* because he does not know how to spell them.
— he had written "determain" because he thought it sounded like *remain*. This was a conscious effort to use a known spelling in order to come up with a possible spelling for an unfamiliar word.

Dan was not aware that he had a problem with doubling. Knowing that doubling a consonant makes the previous vowel short may correct his spelling of *writting*, and help with many other words.

Dan needs to learn to make meaning connections.
— he did not know that he confused *were* and *where*. Awareness of these words may help him to proofread for this particular error.
— he was able to spell *busy* with no problem, but had never connected it with *business*. It had never occurred to him to connect words in this way.
— he had no memory of *mediocre*, so made a prediction which could be read. Dan was advised to link "medi" with "mini" and "maxi". He immediately recognized the meaning link among these three words. *Ocre* is uncommon, and needs to be memorized.
— "cayous" was another invention. He was fascinated to see *chaos* written down, and interested in the Greek origin. He was also shown *chasm, choir, chorus, chameleon* and *character* as a rare spelling group.
— he had written "conquere" to rhyme with *were*. He learned that "er" is a verb function ending, as in *canter, wonder*, and a more common ending than "ere", such as in *sister, water, teacher.*
— *personel* is a word he has probably seen more often than *personal*. Correct pronunciation of these two might help him to remember the difference. He made up his own mnemonic device — a person called Al.

Dan was also advised to ask a friend to help with proofreading important pieces, such as a letter of application to a university.

Dan was excited by talking about his writing and the analysis of his spelling patterns, and felt empowered by his new learning. He could now proofread and look for some specific errors, and had learned new ways to figure out and remember spellings. Above all, he had learned that there are strategies for making decisions about spellings.

Dan is a keen writer. He kept a journal on his 46-day trip to Alaska. When writing for himself as an audience he was more relaxed and made fewer spelling errors. Talking about his successes and his errors seemed to open new doors for Dan. He gave us permission to reprint his letter because of a desire to reach out to others who may have a similar problem. He has made a commitment to being accurate in his written English. We wish him well.

When we are looking at samples of student writing our first reaction is often to ask the age or grade level of the writer. This is because we have certain expectations, or norms, against which we judge the worth of the composition, handwriting, spelling, complexity of language, level of vocabulary, and so on. Knowing how a student ranks among others of the same age may well be valid for certain purposes, but for assessing the progress of an individual, or deciding what kind of help a student needs it is less than useful.

To help both teacher and student, information about spelling must be specific and detailed. *Knowing the kind of errors a student makes is more useful than knowing how many mistakes.* Just as the student will learn about spelling by recognizing patterns and making generalizations, so the teacher can help by assessing which patterns and generalizations the student is familiar with, and which need to be taught. Spelling errors, other than typographical ones done in the course of a hasty draft, are not usually made at random — some logic is used to arrive at a particular combination of letters. Analyzing spelling miscues can be a window on a student's understanding of the logic of spelling.

Anecdotal Records

An anecdotal record is a kind of journal you keep about the

students. In your journal you can record your observations and impressions in more detail and with more personal input than you can on a checklist. Your journal is a place for reflections, opinions, hypotheses, and predictions rather than just facts and information.

You may wish to take a little time each day or week to update your journal; you might prefer to keep it handy beside you so you can note down anything significant at the time you notice it. Your journal entries can help you to build up a picture of what a student knows, how a students feels, and how a student works. You might include observations like these:

- Behaviors you notice while you are observing a student at work.
- Evidence of spelling learning you see in a student's writing.
- Particular problems a student is encountering.
- Comments other teachers make about a student's spelling.
- A record of spelling points you have discussed in a writing conference.
- A record of any communication you have with parents.
- Recommendations for instruction or help.

Here are some hints to get you started:

- If you are not an experienced observer, make yourself a list of behaviors and attitudes you would like to look for. Keep it beside you as a guide:
    - is relaxed while writing.
    - uses invented spelling to write unfamiliar words.
    - does not worry about spelling at early stages of writing.
    - understands when spelling matters.
    - can usually find words in a dictionary.
    - sees spelling errors as learning possibilities.
    - knows how to use a cheat sheet.

Add more features to your list as you discover them.

- Set up a binder with a page for each student. Add more pages as you need them. Add writing samples which illustrate your comments.
- Keep the binder near you, or in a place where you read and talk to students about their writing. After a conference, it doesn't take a moment to jot down your thoughts and observations.
- Date all your entries.

- Keep your entries short and quick. You are not writing for an audience. If your journal becomes time-consuming you will be tempted to not continue with it.
- Every week or two browse through your journal and bring yourself up to date. Note which students you have written nothing for, and consider why. Take special note of these students in the next day or two.

Checklists

You will want to keep a cumulative record of concepts each student knows and can use, as well as trace growth and development. Checklists are ideal for these purposes:

- Making a checklist can help you identify in your own mind particular skills or concepts you feel are important.
- A checklist can be a ready reminder of the kinds of information you are looking for.
- A checklist can set specific goals for individuals, both students and teachers, and can record specific achievements.
- A checklist can help you group students for specific instruction.
- A checklist does not take a lot of time to fill in.
- You may see patterns emerge as checkmarks cluster in certain areas.
- If you use a date rather than a checkmark, you can record rate of growth.
- Older students can make and keep their own checklists. Every check they make is a record of achievement which can readily be seen.
- Checklists can continue with students throughout the school. Growth can then be traced for more than a ten-month period.

The most useful checklist is the one you make for yourself. In this way your checklists can match what you are teaching, and reflect the age and interests of the students you teach. What follows are some suggestions for checklists to get you started.

Checklist of Spelling Development

For early spellers, you will need a checklist of spelling stages. First a word of caution. All children will not exhibit signs of every stage. Some children progress very rapidly and seem to move towards standard spelling in a few weeks. Sometimes a particular piece of writing will seem to be a regression; if the topic or style are more ambitious, less attention is likely to be paid to spelling and fewer sounds might be represented. No developmental learning progresses in even and continuous steps. Bearing this in mind, a checklist of spelling development will give you a quick guide to each child's progress and level.

First, make for yourself a list of the steps you expect to see in the spelling. For example:

Pictures only to tell a story
Play-writing in scribble
Strings of random letters
Initial consonants to represent whole words
Initial and final consonants
Spaces between words
Some vowels as placeholders
Some vowels sounds represented accurately
All syllables of words represented
A vowel or "y" in each syllable

Print these across the top of a copy of your class list. When you see a child showing signs of a new stage, mark it with a date. You will be able to see at a glance where each child is in terms of development. The checklist will enable you to group children according to stage if you wish, or to make sure you have a mixed grouping for some writing activities.

Checklist of Spelling Concepts

For more advanced spellers, those who have moved past invented spelling, you may wish to keep a record of spelling concepts you have taught or have discussed with a student. You can then look for these in the writing, and note whether a student is able to use them successfully. This list will also indicate to you features a student can be expected to proofread for. The students might also keep their own list of their responsibilities in proofreading. As this list grows, it will show both you and the students what they are learning, and how their knowledge of spelling is growing.

To create your checklist, list all the spelling concepts you can think of that your students might be expected to know. For beginning spellers the list might start with consonant sounds; for older students you might omit the basic phonics and begin at a later stage. As you notice other concepts in the students' writing, add them to your list.

Vowel or "y" in every syllable
Final "e" makes vowel long
Adding "ing"
Changing "y" to "i"
Doubling final consonant
Plurals with "s"
Plurals with "es"
Plurals with "ies"
Contractions
Adding "ly"
Possessives

To update your records of the concepts a student can use, you could use a student's writing portfolio. This is a collection of the student's best work, collected and put in a separate writing folder, perhaps at the end of each month. You can look through these pieces of writing, noting whether they are edited or not, and check the spelling against a list of concepts you could expect the student to know and use. Any spelling concepts you see being correctly applied in the student's writing can be checked off on your list. This can form the basis of your cumulative record of spelling concepts. For other possible concepts to look for, check the chapter on the Las Vegas Rules of Spelling. You can add to this list as you discover new patterns.

You may also like to keep a list for yourself to record what you have taught. This is particularly useful for those times when you capitalize on the moment and teach an unplanned mini-lesson. You could record what you talk about in conferences with individual students, as well as topics you cover with the whole class.

You may also find that recording what you tell students about spelling will give you a growing list of spelling information and concepts. The contexts in which these topics arose will also give you possible teaching ideas which you may be able to recreate another time. This could be invaluable next time you are planning spelling instruction. It is much easier to list concepts and lesson ideas after they have come up in the course of classroom activities, than to plan for them all beforehand. The notes you take this year could form the basis of your day-book next year.

Keeping Parents Informed

About Spelling

The experiences most of us had in our own schooling led us to believe that spelling is a matter of memorizing words and being able to reproduce them on demand. We in the teaching profession now know that this is not the case. Memorization plays a part, but there are many other skills necessary for a person to be a successful speller. If parents are going to support us in our teaching, and be able to help their children, we must communicate the facts of spelling, along with the ways we are helping children grow as spellers.

Here are some facts parents need to know about spelling and spelling instruction:

- Children will learn to spell in the same way they learned to talk — by approximating what they see around them, and gradually getting closer and closer to standard English. In the early stages their spelling will be no more intelligible than was their early babbling. This is normal, and should be encouraged.
- Children learn to spell in order to write. The more writing they do, the more they can learn about spelling. Anything that makes them reluctant to write will work against spelling learning.

- Spelling is a skill of constructing words, not of memorizing words. Therefore children who learn to "invent" spellings know more about our spelling system and are ultimately better spellers than those who have only tried to memorize words.
- Children are learning about spelling even when they are making errors. They do not write letters at random; they reason logically, and use the best information they have to build words. It is by analyzing the errors they make that we know what they need to learn.
- Invented spelling doesn't "stick". Children will not memorize invented spellings and maintain them throughout their lives any more than they retained their baby talk. If they read a lot they will see standard spellings far more often than their invented spellings. From these models, and from the help and instruction we give, children will build up their knowledge of how words are constructed, gradually come closer to standard spelling, and abandon their primitive inventions.
- Good spellers have three main strategies for spelling:

  1. Matching sounds with letters. Many words can be spelled this way. Parts of all words can be spelled this way.
  2. Considering how a word is used. For example, a past tense is spelled "ed" even if it sounds like "id" or "t". (*waited* and *jumped*)
  3. Considering the meaning of a word. For example, you can remember the correct spelling of *here* if you connect it with other words meaning a location—"there", "where". "Please" and "pleasant" have the same vowel combination, even though they are pronounced differently. It is the meaning that gives you the correct spelling, not the sound.

Young children will learn #1 first. Later, they will become increasingly proficient in using the other two strategies to construct words.

- There is a lot to learn about spelling. It will take children many years to learn enough to become reasonably proficient spellers. For a number of years, they will be writing words they cannot spell. Therefore, when we evaluate their spelling learning we are not necessarily looking to see how many words they get right or wrong, but whether they are learning new concepts and spelling patterns.

- Children who are anxious about making spelling errors are reluctant to write. As a result, they learn neither composition nor spelling.
- We recognize the importance of spelling. However, it is only a small part of the total writing process. We teach writing and spelling one skill at a time in order to ensure better learning. Therefore in some pieces of writing, spelling will not be a primary focus; it may not be mentioned at all. At other times, spelling will be a focus, and we will direct students' attention to specific words and concepts.

Remember, your students will communicate more to their parents than you can ever hope to, in their attitudes and their comments. Make sure they understand what they are doing and why at all stages of the writing process. They should be able to explain why spelling has not been corrected in a first draft, or why they sometimes learn to spell only parts of words. It is usually obvious even to a casual observer, what a writer does *not* know about spelling; the students should be able to communicate what they *do* know, and how their spelling awareness is growing.

About Their Children's Progress

What is it parents really want to read about their children on report cards? There are three main questions they want answered:

1. Does the child have a good attitude towards work and learning?
2. Is the child performing at a reasonable level of achievement for his or her age group?
3. Has the child made progress since the last reporting period?

These three points might form the basis of your reporting. They could also provide a framework for any interview you have with the parents or with the student.

To supply this information to parents you need to do the following:

- Observe the students at work and talk to the students about spelling to determine attitudes, methods of working, and so on. You will do this while students are writing, working on spelling activities, or having conferences with you or with one another.

- Keep a cumulative record of concepts the student knows and applies in writing.
- Track growth by dating your cumulative records and by recording progress through developmental stages.

Conclusion

In our introduction, we stressed the importance of balance in our teaching. Along with the confidence to experiment and the freedom to fail, students need help to learn about spelling. Spelling, like all other subjects, has a *content*, as well as methodology. To be successful, most students need *information*, as well as practice.

We have rightly moved away from viewing spelling as a first and major consideration in writing. Perhaps in our eagerness to embrace composition as our major writing focus we have minimized both the importance and the fascination of spelling and language.

If we have a true understanding of the writing process, we can put spelling in perspective both for ourselves and for our students. Once we raise their awareness of the way words are constructed, and of the interrelationship of language and spelling, we can expect that their knowledge of patterns and anomalies will continue to grow and fascinate long after they have left school. That learning will be a lifelong affair is surely the ultimate goal of all teaching.